in my
FOOTSTEPS
a Cape Cod traveler's guide

CHRISTOPHER SETTERLUND

Second Edition

SCHIFFER
PUBLISHING

4880 Lower Valley Road • Atglen, PA 19310

Library of Congress Control Number: 2022947286

Cover design by Justin Watkinson
Type set in Helvetica Neue/BauerBodni/Gotham

ISBN: 978-0-7643-6667-3
Printed in China

Published by Schiffer Publishing, Ltd.
4880 Lower Valley Road
Atglen, PA 19310
Phone: (610) 593-1777; Fax: (610) 593-2002
Email: Info@schifferbooks.com
Web: www.schifferbooks.com

For our complete selection of fine books on this and related subjects, please visit our website at www.schifferbooks.com. You may also write for a free catalog.

Schiffer Publishing's titles are available at special discounts for bulk purchases for sales promotions or premiums. Special editions, including personalized covers, corporate imprints, and excerpts, can be created in large quantities for special needs. For more information, contact the publisher.

We are always looking for people to write books on new and related subjects. If you have an idea for a book, please contact us at proposals@schifferbooks.com.

CONTENTS

INTRODUCTION

For most visitors, Cape Cod probably brings to mind some common themes: beaches, clam chowder, and whale watches, to name a few. This is what most people think of when they think of Cape Cod, and usually is what their visiting experience encompasses.

For me, Cape Cod is in my blood; it is my family. I am a twelfth-generation Cape Codder with lineage dating back to the seventeenth century. The most-well-known names in Cape Cod history (Doane, Nickerson, Wixon, Chase, and Crowell) are sprinkled throughout my family tree. I have been to every nook and cranny of this great area and want to share with you some places you know and many that you may not. These places, their stories, and their history are what make Cape Cod such a unique place to live and visit.

This travel guide is designed to make visiting Cape Cod as convenient as possible. The sites to see are all in geographical order as one would see them, beginning with the trip over the Sagamore Bridge. This approach will help any visitor see as many beautiful spots on the Cape while conserving time and gas. Have fun and happy traveling!

A VIEW OF THE SAGAMORE BRIDGE FROM THE MAINLAND SIDE OF THE CAPE COD CANAL

Note: At the time of publication, all fees and regulations were accurate. They are subject to change.

I

SANDWICH

GPS: (41.772272, -70.492512)
Address: 93 Town Neck Road

1. First Beach

The eastern mouth of the Cape Cod Canal is reached by taking a drive down Town Neck Road to Sandwich's First Beach. There is a very rocky beach between the parking area and the breakwater of the canal. The waves pull at the rocks, creating a crackling sound that can be hypnotic at times. From the breakwater, one can see straight across to Scusset Beach in Sagamore. It is often possible to see vessels, both large and small, pass by this spot as they go through the

A SHIP EXITING THE EASTERN MOUTH OF THE CAPE COD CANAL

canal and head out into Cape Cod Bay. At a maximum width of 540 feet, the canal carries more than 20,000 ships through its waters annually. It was opened on a limited basis in 1914 and finished in 1916, although the idea of a canal in the area was originally pondered by Myles Standish as early as 1623. Since the canal was not around a hundred years ago, towns such as Wareham, on the northern shore of the canal, consider themselves to be part of the Cape.

A trail leads from the eastern end of the canal at the bay to the Sandwich Marina. This is an active place used by pleasure craft, fishermen, lobstermen, and the US Coast Guard, whose station is nearby. The Cape Cod Canal Visitor Center is also nearby, at 60 Ed Moffitt Drive. It is run by the Army Corps of Engineers. On the other side of the marina is Canal Generating Plant. This is the perfect place to begin a walk, run, or bike ride along the canal.

Important Info:
- Daily parking: $20
- No lifeguard or concessions
- Dogs allowed Labor Day–Memorial Day

2. Town Neck Beach and the Sandwich Boardwalk

Town Neck Beach and the Sandwich Boardwalk are a little difficult for the novice to find; the only sign for the boardwalk is a thin, white pole on Jarves Street just off Rt. 6A with "Boardwalk" and an arrow pointing you in the right direction.

Once you have found it, however, this spot is incredible; nearly all of the boards that make up the walkway are adorned with messages. From memories of 9/11 to good wishes for America, from local business names to couples celebrating their love, the boardwalk in Sandwich is less of a way to reach the beach than a slice of American life. It is tempting to stop and read each of the messages adorning the 1,000 feet of boards that carry you across the marsh.

As you follow the boardwalk, you will have some tremendous views of the natural life in the surrounding salt marsh ecosystem. The view of the actual beach is astounding as well. The boardwalk leads you up a dune where you can see the nearby Cape Cod Canal and across the water to Sagamore Beach and Plymouth. Visitors can walk the boardwalk, reading the messages on each plank, then relax on a beautiful beach with a great view.

The first boardwalk was constructed in 1875 by Gus Howland. Due to many severe storms over the years, the current boardwalk will be replaced by a new, wider, and, it is hoped, more durable one by fall 2023.

Important Info:
- Daily parking $20
- No lifeguard or concessions
- Dogs allowed Labor Day–Memorial Day

TOWN NECK BEACH IN SANDWICH

THE BOARDWALK AT BOARDWALK
BEACH IN SANDWICH

Town Neck Beach & Boardwalk Beach
Sandwich

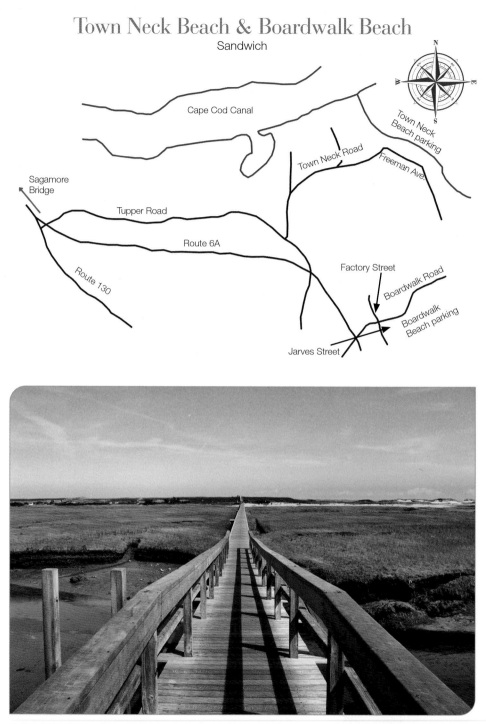

THE BOARDWALK AT BOARDWALK BEACH IN SANDWICH

3. Shawme-Crowell State Forest

Shawme-Crowell State Forest gets its name from the Native Americans, who called the area around Sandwich "Shawme." It can be entered from two directions: trails will be found across the street from the Heritage Museum & Gardens off Grove Street, or you can use the main entrance on Rt. 130.

The forest offers a great hike through more than 700 acres of forest. It has a year-round campground with 285 sites available and is filled with lots of picnic areas providing tremendous views of the pine forest.

The trails leading from Grove Street have clever names such as the Coyote Den, Raccoon Den, Sherris Berries, and Mayflower Trails. They parallel the highway at spots, so it is difficult to get lost.

The main entrance features roads with letter names—Road A, for example—which make them easy to follow. There is a playground for the children on Road C next to the Friends Pavilion, deep inside the forest, which can be used for larger gatherings. There are more than 15 miles of roads and trails to be walked. Often visitors will see horseback riders going from one old dirt fire road to another. It is easy to spend an entire day wandering Shawme-Crowell State Forest, even if you are not camping out.

Important Info:
- Free entrance
- Camping: $17 per night for Massachusetts residents; $54 per night for nonresidents

THE FRIENDS PAVILION

THE MAIN ROAD INTO SHAWME-CROWELL STATE FOREST

4. Heritage Museum & Gardens

This is a perfect way to spend a day on Cape Cod. Heritage Museum & Gardens has so much to see and do.

The land was first settled in 1677 by Lydia Wing Hamilton Abbott. To this day the Wing family farm makes up part of the Heritage grounds.

Among the exhibits is the J.K. Lilly Automobile Museum, which is in a beautiful, round, Shaker stone barn and contains more than thirty classic vehicles. The more well known are a 1913 Ford Model T, Gary Cooper's Duesenberg, and President William H. Taft's parade vehicle. There is also an American History Museum and the Old East Windmill. The windmill was built in Orleans in 1800. It was sold to Heritage in 1968 and painstakingly moved 32 miles to its current location. There are often temporary exhibits in addition to the permanent collection.

A GARDEN AT HERITAGE MUSEUM & GARDENS.

The gardens here are spectacular, encompassing 100 acres and including labeled trees and shrubs, specially designed gardens, and large lawns. These gardens are perfect in any season.

The Heritage Museum & Gardens are typically open May 1 to October 31 from 10 a.m. to 5 p.m. It is important to call ahead or check their website, though, to be certain. It offers an amazing collection of American history and a beautiful natural environment that all visitors to Cape Cod should take the time to see.

Important Info:
- Admission: adults: $22; youth (3–17) $12; children 2 and under free, members free

THE ENTRANCE TO HERITAGE MUSEUM & GARDENS

J.K. LILLY AUTOMOBILE MUSEUM

5. Sandwich Historic Center

Cape Cod has many historic places, and each town has a historic center. Sandwich is the oldest town on the Cape, and its historic center should be the first one you visit. There is no shortage of parking places.

Hoxie House, at 18 Water Street, is as good a place as any to begin a walk through town. The house dates to 1675 and was the home of Reverend John Smith and his large family. This traditional "saltbox"-style house is the oldest of this type on Cape Cod. It was purchased by Capt. Abraham Hoxie in the mid-nineteenth century, which is how it got its name. It is surprisingly one of few historic homes on the Cape in its original location, since so many have been moved to other locations in an attempt to preserve them. It is typically open for tours from June through September, but check before going.

A few houses away is the Thornton W. Burgess Museum. Located in the Deacon Eldred House, built in 1756, this museum is dedicated to Burgess, an author and creator of such beloved children's book characters as Peter Rabbit. The museum is open from approximately Memorial Day to Columbus Day.

Continue walking past the Burgess Museum to see some panoramic views of Shawme Pond. On the edge of the pond is another historic site, Dexter's Grist Mill, which still operates today and offers freshly ground cornmeal for sale inside. The mill was built in 1654 and restored in 1961. Thomas Dexter, for whom it is named, began building gristmills on the site in 1637, to grind grain into flour and meal. The water turns the wooden wheel of the mill, then continues under the street.

There is a running spring next to the stone wall that borders the mill grounds. People come from all over to fill their water jugs with its fresh water.

As you walk around town you will enjoy many historic, well-maintained homes and businesses. It is a great place to park and take a leisurely walk through the oldest town on Cape Cod: Sandwich.

Important Info:
- Hoxie House/Dexter Grist Mill combo admission: adults, $5; children, $3
- Burgess Museum: admission by donation

HOXIE HOUSE

THORNTON BURGESS MUSEUM

DEXTER'S GRIST MILL

NEWCOMB TAVERN, SANDWICH

6. Wing Fort House

Not only is this the oldest house on Cape Cod, but it is the oldest house in Massachusetts continuously owned by the same family. It was built in 1641 by John Wing after he moved to Sandwich in 1637–38, and has been in the Wing family ever since. It is thought that it was known as the Fort House due to it perhaps being used as shelter from Native American attacks. Both the house and Wing Memorial History Center next door are open to the public for tours during the season.

Important Info:
• For more tour info, check out WingFamily.org

WING FORT HOUSE IN SANDWICH

GPS: (41.738528, -70.381318)
Address: Sandy Neck Road

7. Sandy Neck Beach & Sandy Neck Trails

Sandy Neck Beach is one of the most popular beaches on the Cape. The beach can be quite rocky closer to the water but is so large that finding a comfortable spot is not difficult. The famed dunes of Sandy Neck have long been protected by locals. As far back as the 1700s, measures were put in place to keep the dunes from eroding. Farmers were told not to allow their herds to graze there, and whaling ships anchored offshore were limited in the wood they could take from the Sandy Neck area for their boilers.

Directly across from the ranger station on Sandy Neck Road is a sign for the Sandy Neck Nature Trails. There are six walking trails of varying distances, a horse trail, a beach access trail, and some connectors. Should you choose, you can walk more than 6 miles east, ending at a strip of seaside homes and the lighthouse opposite Barnstable Harbor. Even if you don't go the full distance, the Sandy Neck Trails have some amazing natural beauty and a few pieces of history as well. You start out on the Beach Access Trail, which goes along the beach. With permits, this is open to off-road vehicles at certain times of the year. The Marsh Trail breaks off to the right and follows the border of the dunes and the salt marsh, moving east. The salt marsh is on the right, complete with several small birdhouses and an osprey nest situated on top of a pole out in the marsh.

Staying on the Marsh Trail, after Trail 1 breaks off to the left and heads to the bay you will start to see the larger dunes that Sandy Neck is known for, with even better views farther along. Keep walking along the Marsh Trail and you will notice the first of many small cottages, most of them a hundred years old, that dot the land. These are great reminders of what Sandy Neck was like in the early twentieth century, when it was part of the fishing and whaling industry. The cottages are usually occupied in the summer, so be respectful of their property.

For the most part, until you reach Trail 2 the land is uniform—mainly beach sand. The majestic dunes are in plain sight the entire time. Once you pass Trail 2 and a small guard shack just off the trail, the land begins to change a bit. There are still mountainous dunes, but trees become more abundant, as do the fishing cottages. There is no Trail 3, so take Trails 2 or 4 for beach access. Trail 4 will lead you through the dunes and spotty trees and vegetation to the beach and offers a tremendous view.

Branching off Trail 4 is a trail designated for horseback riding, but it is obviously also fine for human use. This trail takes you winding through the trees, and, if not for the constant hum of the ocean waves, you might forget that a beach is close by. There are many tiny ponds scattered throughout this area, but swimming in them is probably not possible, or recommended.

This area of Sandy Neck is also rich in wildlife. Many species of birds, including hawks and osprey, will fly by. On the ground the most-common animals spotted are squirrels, but raccoons, skunks, and an occasional deer can also be seen.

As the Marsh Trail becomes Trail 5, it weaves its way through the trees and will take you out to the beach. It is here that you may go left and head back to the parking lot or continue on to Trail 6 and the tip of Sandy Neck. It is a long walk, but the views are incredible. The cottages, marsh, dunes, trees, ponds, trails, and lighthouse all make for an amazing hike.

Important Info:
- Daily parking: $25
- Lifeguard and concessions in season
- ORV seasonal pass: nonresident: $160
- Dogs allowed Labor Day–Memorial Day

A COTTAGE ALONG THE SANDY NECK TRAILS

THE FAMED DUNES AT SANDY NECK

II

WEST BARNSTABLE
& CUMMAQUID

GPS: (41.688751324623034, -70.3957819914686)
Walker Deck Overlook (41.69911555256256, -70.41838099159001)
Address: Popple Bottom Road, Marstons Mills

1. West Barnstable Conservation Area

This 1,200-acre parcel of land is filled with trails for hiking and mountain biking. The 21-mile mountain biking network was once called the Trail of Tears, but improvements to the terrain have made that name a misnomer today. The crown jewel for hikers is the Walker Point Deck. The view from it is spectacular, since at 232 feet it is the highest point in Barnstable. There are dozens of trails, making any hike unique by choosing different routes. Hunting is allowed at times on this property, so it is wise to be aware of your surroundings.

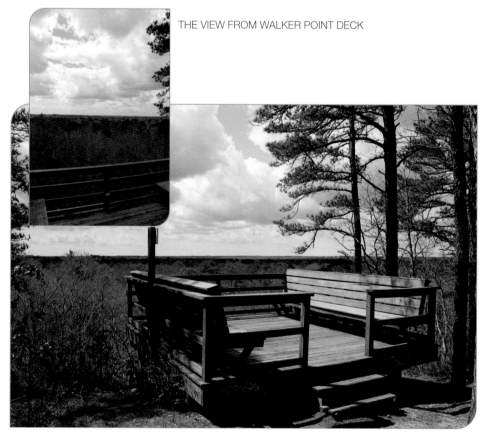

THE VIEW FROM WALKER POINT DECK

WALKER POINT DECK IN WEST BARNSTABLE

2. Cape Cod Airfield

This 80-acre grassy airfield is home to rides in a replica 1930s red biplane, skydiving, and more. If being up in the sky does not appeal to you, it is just as rewarding to sit in your car and watch the planes coming and going and the skydivers floating down to earth. There are also picnic tables and chairs for a closer view. The airfield dates to the 1920s and today is home to twenty-one private planes. It was once a training field for the Army Air Corps, and legend has it that Amelia Earhart once landed there.

It is a popular family activity, especially during the summer months, so call ahead to make an appointment. They do not take appointments via email.

Important Info:
• Free parking; biplane rides: 15 mins., $200; 25 mins., $250; 35 mins., $325

3. Coast Guard Heritage Museum & Old Jail
West Barnstable

With the Coast Guard's connection to Cape Cod and its history, it is only natural that there is a Coast Guard Heritage Museum located here. It is at Cobb's Hill, opposite the Unitarian Church of West Barnstable. The museum opened in 2005 in a building that was once a United States customs house. Hours are 10 a.m. to 3 p.m., Tuesday to Saturday, from May through mid-October.

Located on the grounds of the Coast Guard Heritage Museum, another piece of Cape Cod and American history is known as the "Oldest Wooden Jail in America." The Old Jail is purported to have been built in the 1690s and was in use until a new stone jail was built around 1820.

The jail was situated on private property on Old Jail Lane, just west of the Coast Guard Heritage Museum, until 1972. The owner thought it was an old barn. Thankfully she brought Barnstable Country chief deputy sheriff Louis Cataldo to view the "barn." In 1949 Cataldo had founded Tales of Cape Cod, a repository of Cape history. When he realized what the barn really was, he made it a mission to save it and move it.

The Old Jail is open Tuesdays, Thursdays, and Saturdays from May through mid-November. It is a hidden gem of Cape history. After walking through the Old Jail, a drive down narrow, secluded Old Jail Lane is recommended as well. It is a perfect capper to the experience.

Important Info:
- Coast Guard Museum: admission $5; children under 10 are free
- Old Jail: free admission, donations welcome

COAST GUARD HERITAGE MUSEUM

THE OLD JAIL

GPS: (41.708972, -70.27672)
Address: 345 Bone Hill Road, Cummaquid

4. Long Pasture Wildlife Sanctuary
Cummaquid

This 110-acre wildlife sanctuary is filled with trees and flowers and a couple of small ponds. Located on Bone Hill Road, there are two entrances to Long Pasture. The first is a small, rocky parking lot on the left side, at the first turn of the narrow road. The pathway from this parking area is clearly marked and simple to follow. The second, main entrance is a few hundred yards farther at the large white Sanctuary sign on the left; the road will take you to the visitors parking area.

A few hundred feet into the wooded area there is a small open barn with temporary pens used during the warmer months. This area is part of a cooperative effort between the Massachusetts Audubon Society and Ocean Song Farm to attempt something called "management intensive grazing." The farm's pigs, goats, sheep, and turkeys are there to feed on the vegetation at Long Pasture, which is not treated with pesticides. The animals are fun to see, but be careful: the fences are electrified.

The Long Pasture Wildlife Sanctuary Nature Center has extensive views across Barnstable Harbor toward Sandy Neck Colony and the lighthouse at the end of the Sandy Neck Trails. The Nature Center is open year-round, offering a variety of experiences depending on the time of day and season of the year.

After visiting the nature center, you can return to the parking area at the beginning of Long Pasture by going back the way you came or taking the pathway that runs along Bone Hill Road itself. Separated from the road by a short rock wall, the hike back along Bone Hill Road is nearly as quiet and peaceful as the wooded pathway. The road is not busy, even in the summer months, allowing the birds' songs to be heard all around you. The hike does not end there, though. On the left side of Bone Hill Road, just after the intersection with Harbor Point Road, there are a few perfectly manicured meadows to be walked. In the summer the meadow grasses grow high and the paths become hidden from the roads. In the cooler months the meadows are wide open and easily found.

Important Info:
- Admission: $4 adult, $3 seniors and children ages 3–12

GOATS AT LONG PASTURE

Long Pasture & View of Sandy Neck Colony

Cummaquid

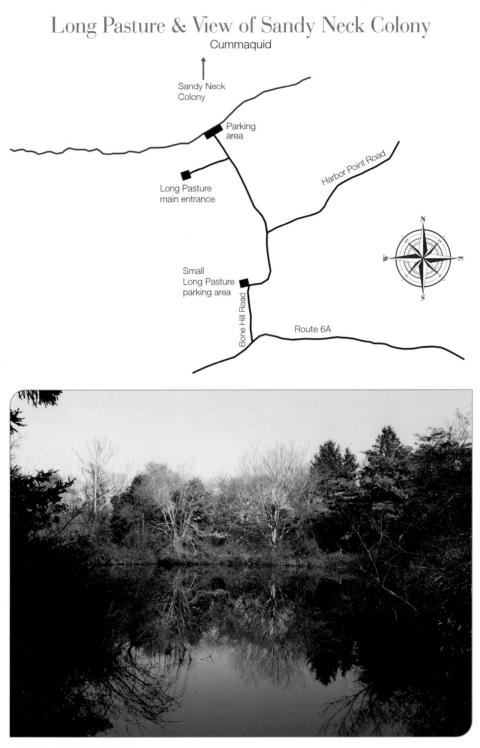

Sandy Neck Colony

Parking area

Long Pasture main entrance

Harbor Point Road

Small Long Pasture parking area

Bone Hill Road

Route 6A

N
W E
S

A POND AT LONG PASTURE

5. View of Sandy Neck Colony
Cummaquid

The Sandy Neck Colony is a small group of cottages and a lighthouse at the tip of 4,700-acre Sandy Neck Beach. Access to this area is limited to boat travel, off-road vehicles, and those brave enough to walk the 7 miles each way in the sand. However, there are a number of places where this small community can be seen and enjoyed from afar.

One is a tiny, sandy parking area at the end of Bone Hill Road, off Rt. 6A, in Cummaquid. This area, next to the Massachusetts Audubon Long Pasture Wildlife Sanctuary, is almost directly across from the cluster of cottages and provides perhaps the best view, aside from being on the opposite shore. This area is quite secluded, with room for about four vehicles in the parking area. When the tide is low, one can walk to the edge of the still water and feel like you can almost touch the other shore.

Because of Sandy Neck Colony the beach has been designated a historic district. After being shut down since 1952, the lighthouse was recently reactivated in 2007, in time to celebrate the lighthouse's 150th anniversary. It was built in 1857 and was repainted a vibrant white in 2021.

Important Info:
- Free but limited parking
- No lifeguard or concessions

SANDY NECK COLONY AND LIGHTHOUSE

VIEW OF THE SANDY NECK COLONY FROM BONE HILL ROAD

III

YARMOUTH PORT

1. Hallet's Store

Established in 1889 by Thatcher Taylor Hallet, this Cape institution was originally a pharmacy complete with soda fountain and lunch counter. Now owned by Charles Clark, Thatcher's great-grandson, Hallet's is still serving ice cream and sodas while doubling as a museum. The 120-plus-year-old shop still has all of its original fixtures inside and, when you sit down to have a sandwich, ice cream, or a soda, you are transported back to the late nineteenth century. The dedication to retaining authenticity is what makes Hallet's special. It is open from April through November, but check before going since hours have changed in recent years.

In addition to having food and beverages, Charles Clark has created a museum upstairs. Focusing on the Hallet family through photographs, objects, and memorabilia, this museum is a reflection of a long period in the life of the whole Yarmouth Port community. It is a great experience to enjoy some refreshment and history at this legendary Cape Cod institution.

Important Info:
• Free parking on Rt. 6A

HALLET'S STORE

2. Captain Bangs Hallet House

In an area filled with historic homes, this is one that stands out. Built in 1840 and named for an illustrious nineteenth-century fisherman, it is the only historic house that is regularly open to visitors. Tours of the house take place often during summer and fall, but the grounds are always open to walkers. The house itself is preserved as though it were still the nineteenth century and the captain was expected to return from a voyage at any time. Interestingly, in 1863 Hallet "swapped" homes with another famous captain, Allen Hinckley Knowles. Captain Hallet and his wife lived in Knowles's house until his death in the late nineteenth century.

Behind the Bangs Hallet House is a natural wonder: an English weeping beech tree that is more than a century old. In the warmer months this giant's limbs, covered in broad, flat leaves, reach to the ground. When you step beneath this awesome piece of nature, it feels as if you are under an umbrella. Nature lovers and history buffs alike find that the Hallet House is a great place to spend some time.

Important Info:
• Admission: adults, $10; children and members free

CAPTAIN BANGS HALLET HOUSE

3. Edward Gorey House

The home of this American illustrator, author, playwright, and more is a popular museum today. Gorey lived in the house from 1979 to his death in 2000. In addition to other works, Gorey might be most well known for his artwork in the intro to the PBS *Mystery!* series. There are revolving exhibits and many pieces of memorabilia on display inside. Some of the featured eclectic pieces of Gorey's personality include a month's worth of checks from the iconic Jack's Outback restaurant that was just up the street. The museum is opened year-round, with longer hours in the summer months.

Important Info:
* Admission: adults: $8.00; students & seniors (65+): $5.00; children 6–12 years old: $2.00. Children under 6 are free.

THE EDWARD GOREY HOUSE MUSEUM

EDWARD GOREY'S WARDROBE INSIDE THE MUSEUM

4. Grays Beach (Bass Hole)

Although formally named Grays Beach, this free, public beach nestled against a narrow cove overlooking Cape Cod Bay is known by locals as "Bass Hole." Its Native American name, "Hockanom," means "hook shaped," and legend has it that the Algonquin Native Americans fought Thorvald Ericson, brother of Leif, in 1003 and killed him here.

Any trip here would have to start with the over 800-foot-long boardwalk, which stretches into neighboring Center Street Marsh. It gives a wonderful view of the bay and Chapin Beach, which acts as a barrier protecting Bass Hole from the harsh ocean waves. In recent years, though, erosion from nearby Sandy Neck has choked the waterway in between Chapin and Bass Hole. This makes it possible to walk across at low tide, but caution is advised. The beach area is calm and good for swimming; there are visible sandbars at low tide. A large, open field and a newly revamped playground provide spaces for recreation, and a covered picnic area can be reserved for large parties.

Across from the field are trails that extend through the woods surrounding Bass Hole and across a marsh, which, thanks to a recently built walking bridge, give a great panoramic view of the area. Trails lead through the woods and across Center Street, coming out on the other side of the marsh. There are a lot of biting greenhead flies in late summer, but it should not stop visitors from enjoying one of the few free beaches on Cape Cod.

Important Info:
- $20
- Lifeguard in season
- No concessions

GRAYS BEACH SUNSET ON THE BOARDWALK AT BASS HOLE

5. Taylor-Bray Farm

Tucked away on the north side of Route 6A in Yarmouth Port is this charming small farm. It was originally started by the Taylor Family in the 1640s. The property remained in the family until being sold to the Bray family in 1896. This spot has no shortage of great photo opportunities. From a boardwalk leading to views over the marsh, to various species of animals such as sheep, goats, donkeys, and Scottish cattle, all one has to do is walk the grounds and let the scenes unfold before you. It is 22 acres of serenity.

In 2022 the property's barn underwent extensive renovations. It is also possible to hold events such as birthday parties at the farm.

Important Info:
• Free admission and parking. Donations are appreciated.

IV

DENNIS &
EAST DENNIS

1. Chapin Beach
Dennis

Chapin Beach is named for real estate broker George Chapin, who gave the land to the town just after World War II. Before it was a public beach it was known as "Black Flats," for the color of the sand. Today it offers a different sort of thrill: off-roading. The route to Chapin Beach is nearly 2.5 miles long, leading to a secluded parking lot, though in summer it is extremely crowded. Those vehicles with the capability may opt to drive along the beach, which extends out to where the Chase Garden Creek salt marsh empties into Cape Cod Bay. From there you have a great view of both Sandy Neck in Sandwich to the west and nearby Grays Beach, also known as Bass Hole, to the east.

Chapin Beach acts as a "barrier beach" for Bass Hole, protecting it from most harsh ocean waves. In recent years, though, erosion from nearby Sandy Neck has choked the waterway in between Chapin and Bass Hole. This makes it possible to walk across at low tide, though caution is advised. The drive on Chapin Beach Road is nearly as good as the beach itself. It is a winding, hilly, and sometimes sand-covered journey past beachfront homes with scenic glimpses of Cape Cod Bay. At low tide the beach allows one to walk up to a mile out onto tidal flats; it is one of the best spots to watch a Cape Cod sunset.

Important Info:
- Parking $20 weekdays, $25 weekends and holidays
- No lifeguards
- Concessions
- Dogs allowed Labor Day–Memorial Day

CHAPIN BEACH

2. Scargo Tower
Dennis

Originally built of wood as an observatory for tourists in 1874, Scargo Tower was named for the legendary Nobscusset Indian, Princess Scargo. She was so beautiful, legend has it, that Indian warriors would come from all parts of Cape Cod to see her and bring gifts to help sustain her people. The original tower was destroyed in a storm two years after it was built; it was rebuilt of wood but burned to the ground in 1900. The current stone structure was built in 1901. It was completely restored in 2020.

Standing 30 feet high on top of Scargo Hill, it offers some of the best views of the Mid-Cape area. Cape Cod Bay is easily visible to the north, and Scargo Lake lies at the bottom of the hill. The paths down to the lake have been fenced off, but not too many years ago it was possible to scale the hill down to the shore of the lake. On clear days it is possible to see all the way to Provincetown and Plymouth. The tower and its story are unique in an area that should be visited at least once.

Important Info:
• Free parking/admission

SCARGO TOWER

SCARGO LAKE AS SEEN FROM SCARGO TOWER

3. Nobscusset Indian Burial Site
Dennis

A little hard to find but well worth the stop, this gem of history harkens back to the original Native American inhabitants of Cape Cod. The burial site of the Nobscusset tribe, which inhabited Dennis hundreds of years ago, sits just across the street from Osprey Lane, along Rt. 6A. There is a sign pointing to its location, but it is very easy to miss it and pass by this site altogether. There is no parking area for visitors, but the site is not large and will not take too long to see it, so parking along Osprey Lane should be fine. If parking is not available there, a Town Way to Water lot is only a few hundred yards away on Rt. 6A.

After walking through a natural tunnel of trees, you come upon the burial ground. The tunnel is remarkable, especially when the sun trickles through the branches. The grounds are fenced and marked by a stone stating that the chief of the tribe was named "Mashantampaine." At the back end of the burial ground, the site offers a view of Scargo Lake, but there are many other places with better access to the lake. This tribute to the original inhabitants of Cape Cod should be seen by all visitors.

Important Info:
• Free but limited parking across the street on Osprey Lane

NOBSCUSSET INDIAN BURIAL SITE

Nobscussett Indian Burial Grounds
Dennis

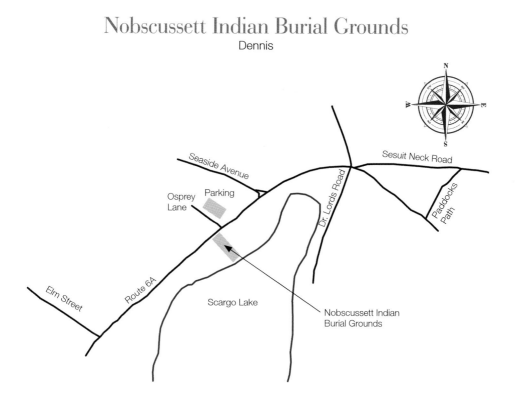

Seaside Avenue

Sesuit Neck Road

Osprey Lane

Parking

Dr. Lords Road

Paddocks Path

Elm Street

Route 6A

Scargo Lake

Nobscussett Indian
Burial Grounds

4. Cold Storage Beach

The eastern side of Sesuit Harbor is home to this popular stretch of beach. The breakwater lining the harbor allows for tremendous vantage points of the boats entering and leaving. It is possible to walk the beach from the edge of the harbor east to Quivett Neck, more than a mile and a half away. The beach got its name for the storage buildings in the area, which kept fish cold in the early twentieth century. Cold Storage is one of eleven north-side beaches in the town of Dennis.

Important Info:
• Daily parking $30

5. Crowes Pasture Beach
East Dennis

Visitors who are not willing or able to take the drive out to Cape Cod National Seashore can have the same experience of untouched Cape Cod at Crowes Pasture Beach. The beach is on South Street in Dennis, just before the Brewster line and past Quivett Cemetery on the east side of Sesuit Harbor. The road to Crowes Pasture Beach is long, bumpy, and unpaved; it is recommended that you take it slow or, better yet, have a vehicle capable of four-wheel drive. The scenery is amazing, especially on your first drive out. The 138-acre conservation area has many designated parking areas with views of Cape Cod Bay and neighboring Quivett Creek Marsh. The popular East Dennis Oyster Farm is in this area on Quivett Neck. From the designated parking areas, it is possible to walk to the beach or to Coles Pond, which sits in the northeast section of Crowes Pasture and only a few hundred yards from the ocean.

Though it is somewhat hidden, Crowes Pasture is a place where you can easily spend a day enjoying the solitude and beauty of Cape Cod as it was when the first settlers gazed upon it.

Important Info:
- Free upland parking
- Off-road driving pass: $165 for Massachusetts residents, $330 nonresidents
- No lifeguard
- No concessions
- Dogs allowed on leash

CROWES PASTURE

V

BREWSTER

1. Drummer Boy Park

This park combines a recreation area with a historical site. Drummer Boy Park is a beautiful, open space that, until mid-2012, was a popular dog park. Dogs are no longer allowed here, but there is a playground for children and some interesting historical buildings to be seen.

First and most obvious is Higgins Farm Windmill, a behemoth on a hill that is easily seen from Rt. 6A. It was built in 1795 and moved from its previous location nearby on Ellis Landing Road in 1974. It was donated to Brewster by Mrs. Samuel Nickerson in memory of her husband.

On either side of the smock windmill are buildings of historical interest. An old blacksmith shop is on the right. It dates back to 1867, when it was built by Henry Hopkins on his property on Long Pond Road. On the left is the Harris-Black House, built in 1795. It is one of the few remaining one-room houses left on Cape Cod. It was moved to Drummer Boy Park from Red Top Road and carefully restored in 1983.

With lots of history and plenty of room for play, this park is a great place for a picnic lunch or to spend an afternoon. There is a nice view of Quivett Creek Marsh on the north side of the park.

Important Info:
- Free Parking
- Dogs are no longer allowed

HARRIS-BLACK HOUSE

HIGGINS FARM WINDMILL

GPS: (41.753562, -70.115209)
Address: 869 Route 6A

2. Cape Cod Museum of Natural History & Wing Island

The Museum of Natural History is filled with amazing exhibits featuring local wildlife and ecology. It is open every day during the summer and most days during the spring and fall and is a perfect family destination, being fun and educational. But it is what is behind the museum that truly makes the trip memorable. It is a living example of what the Natural History Museum's exhibits are all about.

Located across Quivett Creek Marsh, and accessible only at low tide, is Wing Island, named for John Wing, the first white settler to live within the boundaries of what was old Harwich in 1656. To get there, follow the John Wing Trail, which begins as a series of boards across the mucky marsh and leads to Cape Cod Bay. The island trail has several openings allowing a broad view of Quivett Creek Marsh and Cape Cod Bay simultaneously.

The land is filled with birds, butterflies, and sweet-smelling flowers during the warmer months and continues to be an amazing place of natural beauty during the winter.

A parking area in front of the museum gives access to trails on the south side of Rt. 6A that cross a marsh and continue into the surrounding woods. The marsh trail leading to Wing Island is submerged during high tide, so check the charts before heading out there or you may have to slosh your way back to the museum grounds through 2 feet of salt water.

This place seems far removed from civilization and is worth the potential for wet shoes.

Important Info:
- Museum admission: adults (13–64), $15; seniors (65+), $12; children (ages 3–12), $7; children (age 2 and under) and members free. The trail to Wing Island is free.

HEADING ACROSS QUIVETT CREEK MARSH TO WING ISLAND

THE VIEW OF CAPE COD BAY FROM WING ISLAND

3. Paine's Creek Beach

This is a small but popular beach on Cape Cod Bay. It is one of the best spots on the north side for sunset viewing. There is also ample opportunity for kayaking either in Paine's Creek or nearby Quivett Creek to the west. The beach is named for the Paine family, descendants of Thomas Paine Jr., who settled the area in the late 1600s. The low number of parking spaces makes it important to arrive early in the summer.

Important Info:
• Parking: $20/day

SUNSET AT PAINE'S CREEK BEACH IN BREWSTER

4. Stony Brook Herring Run & Grist Mill

Stony Brook Herring Run is a popular site for children and adults alike, especially during the spring herring spawn, when the narrow brook is choked with fish close enough to touch. As tempting as that may seem, taking fish from the grounds is not permitted.

It does not have to be spring to enjoy the herring run. Lower Mill Pond empties through the herring run and continues out into Paine's Creek; a series of "fish ladders," a sort of man-made funneling system for the fish, create a constant rush of water, overpowering most other sounds. There is an old wishing well on the grounds, and a walking bridge over the brook allows for tremendous views of the natural beauty no matter what season it is.

Across the street from the herring run is Stony Brook Grist Mill. The original fulling mill was two hundred years old when it burned to the ground in 1871; the current mill was built on the original foundation two years later. It houses a museum and is still in operation, despite being 140 years old, so visitors can purchase fresh cornmeal inside. The mill has an amazing wooden wheel affixed to its side, making it a very popular subject for photographers. A search for the mill on the internet produces dozens of photos of the left side of the mill, with its large waterwheel prominently featured. Behind the mill you may walk to the stone wall that holds back Lower Mill Pond. The stream leading from this spot to the herring run can be so still at times that it is possible to get a perfect mirror image of the mill reflecting in the water.

Important Info:
- Free parking for Herring Run
- Free admission to Grist Mill

STONY BROOK GRIST MILL

STONY BROOK HERRING RUN

5. Ocean Edge Resort and Golf Club

This entire property was once owned by the Nickerson family. At one time a mansion known as Fieldstone Hall stood here. Samuel Nickerson used his vast fortune to have the three-story home built in 1890. The current Nickerson Mansion was built in 1907, after Fieldstone Hall burned down. For decades the property was home to LaSalette Seminary. The Ocean Edge Resort was first opened in 1981. Today the high-class resort includes a golf club, spa, private beach, restaurants, and private villas. The front lawn became a public area for family activities during summer 2021. The restaurants (Ocean Terrace, Linx Tavern) and bar (Ocean Edge Beach Bar) are also open to the public.

THE NICKERSON MANSION AT THE OCEAN EDGE RESORT

THE BEACH BAR AT OCEAN EDGE RESORT

6. Nickerson State Park

Set on 1,900 prime acres, Nickerson State Park houses many kettle ponds formed by glaciers more than 10,000 years ago. Campsites offer breathtaking views and the sweet scents of the pine forest that no words can describe. The park bears the name Roland J. Nickerson in honor of the owner of the land in the late nineteenth century. His mansion is now part of the Ocean Edge Resort and Club in Brewster.

As you hike around Big Cliff Pond or ride through the 8 miles of bike trails, you may feel like you are in the middle of nowhere. In fact there is a trail at the far end of Nook Road that comes within a few hundred feet of the Mid-Cape Highway.

Flax Pond and Big Cliff Pond are the most-popular places for families to visit. Since none of the kettle ponds have streams or rivers to feed them, their water levels fluctuate from year to year. Just a short walk from the main entrance, Flax Pond has canoes to rent. With no current, the water is very safe and easy to navigate for paddler and swimmer alike.

At the end of Flax Pond Road you will find Big and Little Cliff Ponds. At their nearest point the two kettles are separated by about 75 feet, but they never connect. Canoeing is available here, and there are boat ramps available for people coming with their own water transportation. After a short walk up a hill, you arrive at a picnic area with an aerial view of Big Cliff Pond. In summer the view is obscured by plants and trees. At the top of the hill there are cabins for camping.

Just about any parking area along the whole of the park can be the start of an impressive hike. At Nickerson State Park there really is no bad spot to choose. You will have just as much fun if you point yourself in one direction and just go.

A summer's day at Nickerson would not be complete without stopping at Cobies, a popular restaurant on Rt. 6A just before you reach the Nickerson entrance. It has a congenial, casual atmosphere with outside picnic tables and has been serving great fried food since 1948. A visit here can be a perfect way to start or finish your day.

Important Info:

- Free daily admission
- Daily parking fee (charged May 14 through October 30): MA resident $8, nonresident $30
- Camping fees (per night): MA resident, $22; nonresident $70
- No lifeguards, no concessions
- Dogs allowed except in swimming areas

NICKERSON STATE PARK

FLAX POND AT
NICKERSON STATE
PARK

LITTLE CLIFF POND
AT NICKERSON STATE
PARK

BIG CLIFF POND AT
NICKERSON STATE
PARK

VI

ORLEANS

1. Skaket Beach

Skaket Beach offers beautiful sunset views. Located near the curve of the Cape toward the national seashore on the north, there are seemingly endless views of the Cape as well. It is easy to see up the coast all the way to Provincetown to the east and, on a clear day it is possible to see the South Shore of Massachusetts to the west.

The tide is extreme here; when it goes out, the beach appears to go on forever and makes for an easy walk a half mile to the west to Namskaket Marsh. Skaket Beach is close enough to Orleans Center and the Cape Cod Rail Trail that it is possible to spend the entire day there, have a nice dinner nearby, and return to watch an incredible sunset. The parking lot is not large and fills up fast on summer days, especially with spillover from nearby Nauset Beach, so get there early to enjoy the water and the views.

Important Info:
• Daily parking: $30
• Lifeguards and concessions in season

SKAKET BEACH

2. Rock Harbor

A beautiful place for a swim or a sunset photo, Rock Harbor is unique. In the summer, what a visitor notices first are trees spaced out into the harbor to help guide boats into the harbor. This odd sight may cause you to do a double take, but this is part of Rock Harbor's charm. Typically the trees are adorned with regular street signs to reflect the lights of incoming vessels. The trees are removed during the winter.

Walking the beach to the west will take you to a salt marsh, while an eastern walk will take you to Boat Meadow. For those looking for an adventure on the water, fishing charters are run out of Rock Harbor. It is a popular area for watching the sunset, with the sun dipping below the waters on Cape Cod Bay, many times to rapturous applause. There is plenty of parking.

During the War of 1812 this was the site of a British attack that was thwarted by the Orleans Militia. The ship HMS *Newcastle* sat offshore with the intent of burning the village and its vessels but was repelled by the soldiers from Orleans.

In the harbor during the warmer months is the historic CG36500 Motor Lifeboat, built in 1946. This vessel is famous for rescuing the thirty-two-man crew of the tanker *Pendleton* during a dangerous winter nor'easter in February 1952.

Important Info:
• Free parking

THE TREES AT ROCK HARBOR   CG36500 MOTOR LIFEBOAT AT ROCK HARBOR

SUNSET AT ROCK HARBOR

3. Nauset Beach

Named for the Native American tribe that originally inhabited the area, Nauset Beach is one of the best spots to surf on the East Coast and one of the most popular beaches on the Cape. Located where Nantucket Sound and the Atlantic Ocean collide, Nauset Beach has some rough seas and large waves. Even when the tide is low, the waves here are larger than anywhere else along the shores of Cape Cod. Even if you are not a surfer or don't like to swim, taking a walk along Nauset Beach is a must. In the summer the large parking lot fills up quickly, so it is wise to make a journey to Nauset Beach as early as possible.

Listening to waves and watching them crash on the shore is a soothing, almost meditative experience. If you are walking and lose yourself in the moment, you may look up and suddenly find yourself miles from the parking lot.

Many of the east-facing Cape beaches are visited by seals, dolphins, and other marine animals. Seals are the most plentiful, but there is no guarantee that you will see one bobbing up and down in the water, though it is always possible when the weather is warm.

Nauset Beach is also one of the best spots to watch the sunrise. Though it has been ravaged by erosion over the last several years, this spot still holds a special place in the hearts of locals and visitors. There are miles of open beach to be walked, or driven via the ORV trails. If one dares to walk more than 2 miles south, it is possible to come face to face with the nearly century-old wreck of the schooner *Montclair*.

Important Info:
- Daily parking: $30
- Lifeguards and concessions in season
- Dogs: From a point south of Nauset Beach parking lot to Trail 1, dogs are prohibited from May 15 to Labor Day. From a point south of Trail 1 to the Chatham Inlet, all dogs must be on a leash of not more than 30 feet at all times, unless below the high-tide mark, from May 15 through Labor Day. Dogs are prohibited from areas closed to vehicle or human traffic for piping plover protection.

THE WRECK OF THE MONTCLAIR AT NAUSET BEACH

CROSSING THE DUNES TO
NAUSET BEACH

THE ORV TRAIL AT
NAUSET BEACH

NAUSET BEACH

LOOKING SOUTH AT
NAUSET BEACH IN
ORLEANS

VII

EASTHAM

1. Penniman House & Fort Hill

Built in 1867 by whaling Captain Edward Penniman, Penniman House is a testament to the fortune he gained through seven successful whaling voyages. His love for whaling was once depicted by a pair of whale ribs acting as a trellis over the entry to the front yard; those have long since been removed. Situated among some more modern homes along Fort Hill Road, the Penniman House stands out, with its red and yellow colors and Second Empire–style architecture. The Second Empire style, including some French elements, was popular mainly from 1865 to 1880. This was the first house in town with indoor plumbing. Captain Penniman lived here until his death in 1913. The house was completely renovated back to its former glory in 2016.

After a stroll around the grounds of this marvelous mansion, it is only a short drive to the lookout area of Fort Hill. There is a panoramic view of Salt Pond Bay and the Atlantic Ocean, with a trail that leads down to the water and back toward Red Maple Swamp. When standing at the overlook to the north, you can see all the way to Coast Guard Beach, where the large, white Coast Guard building sits high on a hill. On warm days the ocean breeze makes the trail walk amazing. On cold days it can be tough, but the views are worth the potential shivers.

Important Info:
* Free parking at Fort Hill
* Penniman House admission is free, but donations are appreciated

PENNIMAN HOUSE

THE VIEW FROM FORT HILL

2. Eastham Windmill

Easy to pass without notice, the Eastham Town Green is home to the oldest windmill on Cape Cod. Now across from the Town Hall on Rt. 6, this windmill was originally built in Plymouth in 1680 by Thomas Paine of Eastham. It was subsequently moved to Truro in 1770, to Eastham in 1793, and, finally, to its current home in 1808. There is a gazebo behind the windmill, along with a stone trough that is more than a hundred years old. The water pump is locked, but the trough is a nice supplement to the windmill. Its inscription, "Blessed Are the Merciful," is a positive message to take from the park.

The windmill sits near the back of the park, so it is a piece of history that can be overlooked as people drive by on the main road at 40 miles per hour. It is worth the stop though. It is also possible to see the windmill from the Cape Cod Rail Trail, which passes just west of the green. The park is used for events such as craft fairs and concerts during the warmer months.

Important Info:
• Free parking on either side of the park, along the roads

WINDMILL PARK

3. Salt Pond Visitor Center, Cape Cod National Seashore

Though the Cape Cod National Seashore contains more than 43,500 acres of incredible forest, dunes, and coastline, the actual gateway to the seashore is the Salt Pond Visitor Center. It is open every day from 9 a.m. to 4:30 p.m., with longer hours during the summer. Inside, people can learn what the seashore is all about through films and an extensive museum. The salt pond is down a short trail behind the center.

From the visitor center, a short trip by car, bike, or foot takes you to Doane Rock and Coast Guard Beach. As an alternative, the Nauset Bike Trail, only 1.6 miles in length, also goes down to Coast Guard Beach. For walking, the Nauset Marsh Trail, which is 1.5 miles long, is very popular and easy to navigate. One can access the Cape Cod National Seashore through countless roads and beaches, but beginning a journey into this untouched area of natural beauty at the "gateway" at Salt Pond makes it feel more special.

Important Info:
• Free admission

SALT POND VISITOR CENTER

4. Doane Rock

A part of the national seashore, Doane Rock is a deposit left behind by glaciers and is the largest exposed boulder on the Cape. Roughly 15 feet high, it is a reminder of one of the early Cape Cod families. Deacon John Doane settled in Eastham in 1644 and was a holder of many local government offices before helping to settle Eastham. He was so influential that his name was even mentioned by Henry David Thoreau in his writings about Cape Cod in the mid-nineteenth century.

The boulder can be climbed, with caution, of course, and around the boulder there are trails leading throughout the seashore. A short walk from Doane Rock takes you to the site of Doane Homestead, marked by a granite memorial and a small, square clearing. It is impressive that more than 350 years ago, an original Cape Cod family lived on that spot. Perhaps this is especially true for me because they are my ancestors, but one does not have to be related to the Doanes to appreciate it; any history lover will enjoy it.

Important Info:
• Free admission and parking

DOANE ROCK

SITE OF THE DOANE HOMESTEAD

5. Coast Guard Beach

This is consistently ranked one of America's best beaches, though erosion has ravaged this spot over the decades. It is still filled with people during the summer months. The Blizzard of '78 destroyed the 350-space parking lot as well as Henry Beston's iconic Outermost House, drastically changing the layout of the beach. A satellite parking lot is at the Little Creek Shuttle Staging Area; there are signs to direct you to it. During the summer this is typically used to bring people to the beach, now due to the far-smaller parking lot at the beach itself. It is a very popular surfing beach since it faces the harsh Atlantic Ocean. The erosion is so severe and constant that the beach seems to change week to week. The ever-shrinking shoreline does not stop throngs of tourists and locals from visiting though.

Important Info:
• Daily parking: $25/vehicle; $15/bicycle or on foot

THE STATION AT
COAST GUARD BEACH

COAST GUARD BEACH
IN EASTHAM

GPS: (41.859461, -69.952551)
Address: 120 Nauset Light Beach Road

6. Nauset Lighthouse

Originally part of the Chatham Twin Lighthouses, Nauset Light is on a hill overlooking Nauset Light Beach. It was built in Chatham in 1877 and moved to Eastham in 1923. Before this, the Three Sisters Lighthouses guarded the shore for passing vessels. This cast-iron giant was dismantled in 1993, when the rapidly eroding cliff where the lighthouse stood required that it be moved 300 feet west, where it currently stands. It was saved through a tremendous effort by the Nauset Light Preservation Society (NLPS), which was formed in 1993 by a group of concerned Eastham residents. Since its inception the group has contributed substantial amounts of money toward the moving and restoration of the lighthouse; the society now numbers more than eight hundred members in forty states.

During the 1940s, Nauset Lighthouse was painted red and white to match its red-and-white beacon; its color scheme has made it possibly the most well-known lighthouse on Cape Cod. It is widely recognized as being on the Cape Cod Potato Chips bags. Erosion is still a real problem. In 2021, the road servicing cottages behind the lighthouse had to be relocated due to the encroaching bluffs. Views of the lighthouse from Nauset Light Beach, and vice versa, are simply magnificent. During each of my visits I try to find one new, unique angle of Nauset Light and have not been disappointed yet. There is no shortage of photo opportunities at this historic site. It is open Sundays from July through October.

Important Info:
- Parking is at Nauset Light Beach
- Daily parking: $20 per vehicle, $10 for motorcycles, $3 for pedestrians and bicyclists
- Lifeguards in season, no concessions
- No dogs allowed May 15 to Labor Day

NAUSET LIGHTHOUSE

GPS: (41.85879, -69.957299)
Address: Cable Road

7. The Three Sisters Lighthouses

The "Three Sisters" lighthouses can easily be missed by travelers, since they are not on the shores of Cape Cod but are spaced across an open field down the road from Nauset Light Beach. Their story may be the most amazing of all the Cape lighthouses, but it also may be the least known.

THE THREE SISTERS LIGHTHOUSES

The diminutive Three Sisters, each standing only 15 feet tall (as opposed to the 48-foot- tall Nauset Light), originally sat overlooking Nauset Light Beach as far back as 1838. In 1892 the original brick lighthouses were replaced with these wooden structures. Two towers were removed in 1911, eventually becoming part of the Twin Lights Cottage. The final structure was removed in 1923 to make way for Nauset Light. After being removed during the 1920s to make way for Nauset Light, which had been brought up from Chatham, the Three Sisters were separated for decades until the National Park Service repurchased them one by one. In 1983, after seventy-three years apart, the Sisters were reunited in the field where they currently stand. They were restored and placed the same distance apart that they had been when they watched over the Atlantic. Only the middle Sister, the last one that stood over Nauset Light Beach, still has its lantern adorning its top; there was not enough funding to repair the lantern rooms on the other two.

Parking is limited in a new lot built on Cable Road in 2021, where the lighthouses stand. If that is full, it is possible to park and walk either from Nauset High School or at Nauset Light Beach. They are worth the hike.

Important Info:
- Parking: Parking is free, but limited in the new lot. If that lot is full park and walk from either Nauset High School or at Nauset Light Beach

THE MIDDLE "SISTER" OF THE THREE SISTERS LIGHTHOUSES

VIII

WELLFLEET

GPS: (41.878045, -69.987999)
Address: 51 Route 6

1. Wellfleet Drive-In Theater

A relic harkening back to a different era, Wellfleet Drive-In is one of only 321 active drive-in movie theaters left in the United States as of 2020. At the peak of their popularity in the late 1950s, between 4,000 and 5,000 drive-ins were operating in the US. As recently as the early 1980s there were a handful of drive-ins on Cape Cod, including theaters in Dennis, Yarmouth, and Hyannis. The Dennis drive-in site is now overgrown with trees and brush, and the Yarmouth drive-in site is an open field, while the Hyannis drive-in site is now the Festival Plaza shopping center. The original entrance to the Hyannis site is still evident, since it runs behind the former Borders Bookstore and is designated by a row of trees evenly spaced to the right of the building.

With a 100-by-44-foot screen, the Wellfleet Drive-In has been in operation since 1957 and is open from late May through Labor Day. The soundtrack can be played directly through your car stereo, or, if you want a real trip down memory lane, you can hang the mono speaker on your window. Whether reliving their own childhood or seeing a drive-in movie for the first time, this is an experience that visitors must try. You will not forget it.

Important Info:
- Parking is free
- Tickets for shows are as follows: adults, $12; kids, $9
- Concessions

THE WELLFLEET
DRIVE-IN

GPS: (41.912825, -69.972709)
Address: Marconi Station Road

2. Marconi Station & White Cedar Swamp

Part of the national seashore, the Marconi Station site honors Guglielmo Marconi, who, in 1901, oversaw the building of the first transatlantic wireless telegraph station. In 1903, at a place not too far from the current site, President Theodore Roosevelt sent a radio message across the Atlantic to King Edward VII of England. The station was also one of the first to receive radio distress calls from the *Titanic* after it struck the iceberg in 1912.

There is a platform on a hill near Marconi Station that offers a wide view of the Atlantic Ocean and the national seashore lands surrounding the Marconi site. Originally, four 210-foot-tall wooden towers stood in a square around the transmitter building. Due to heavy erosion of the cliffs, the station remained operational for only sixteen years and was closed and dismantled in 1917.

This is an inspiring place for historians. A small-scale model of the original Marconi Station makes it possible to imagine the giant towers visible from all around Wellfleet. During spring 2011, after a rash of severe storms, a pair of bases of the original Marconi Station towers were revealed on the beach below. They are accessible by walking a little more than a mile from Marconi Beach. It is amazing to see the steel and wood from a hundred years ago still intact after spending more than a century under water and sand. Erosion is a major problem, and the encroaching bluffs have continually changed the landscape of this historic site.

As awe inspiring as the Marconi site, scale model, and revealed tower bases may be for historians, there is a place that produces the same feeling for nature lovers just across the parking lot. A mile-long hike into the sandy pine forest will lead you to White Cedar Swamp, which seems so out of place along the beaches and ocean. The land leading up to the swamp is typical Cape Cod terrain, but White Cedar Swamp seems to appear from nowhere. A boardwalk takes you through the area where trees block most of the sun, allowing only trickles of light to splash through to the water. It has a dusky feeling even in midday and is strange and beautiful. This is one of the most highly recommended places to visit on all of Cape Cod.

Important Info:
• Parking is free

WHITE CEDAR SWAMP

THE MARCONI STATION SITE

ONE OF THE ORIGINAL BASES OF THE MARCONI WIRELESS TOWERS

3. Mayo Beach and the Site of the Chequesset Inn

One of the most fascinating places to visit on the Cape may seem like just another slice of ocean, but the story of what once stood on this spot is a remarkable piece of Cape Cod history. The Chequesset Inn was an exclusive luxury resort built in 1902 on the 400-foot Mercantile Wharf. With sixty-two rooms, the resort helped make Wellfleet a tourist destination. In 1934 the rough waters of the harbor claimed the Chequesset Inn, when a cold winter filled the harbor with ice chunks that ravaged the pier's pilings and caused Mercantile Wharf to collapse during a storm. The inn was taken down shortly thereafter, along with the pier.

There is a marker on the curve of Kendrick Avenue designating where the Mercantile Wharf jutted out into the harbor. To the east is Mayo Beach and to the west are the Wellfleeter Condos. An awe-inspiring feeling comes over you at the edge of the water, knowing what was there seventy-five years ago. At low tide it is still possible to see what remains of the pilings that once made up Mercantile Wharf. A trip to this spot should coincide with low tide, or you will not see anything but water. Make it here at the right time and you will catch a glimpse of history rising from the shallows.

Important Info:
- Free parking in a small turnoff (room for one car). Also parking available at Mayo Beach, where daily parking is also free.
- Dogs allowed October 16 to May 31

THE SPOT WHERE THE OLD
CHEQUESSET INN ONCE STOOD

GPS: (41.93268296073106, -70.0690413584069)
Samuel Smith Tavern (41.93268296073106, -70.0690413584069)
Address: 1440 Chequessett Neck Road, Wellfleet

4. Great Island Trail

In the 2020s it is rare to find areas where one feels truly off the grid. This is one such place. Not to be confused with the private community in Yarmouth of the same name, this Great Island is a peninsula that is part of the Cape Cod National Seashore. The tip of the peninsula, known as Jeremy Point, is part of an 8.8-mile trail loop. Though it can be a long and arduous hike in spots, the views of Cape Cod Bay, Wellfleet Harbor, and even the site of Cape Cod's oldest tavern, the Samuel Smith Tavern, make it worthwhile. Be sure to bring sunscreen and bug spray in the warmer months.

Important Info:
• Free parking

5. Bound Brook Island

Though not really an island, Bound Brook Island is another hidden gem on the Outer Cape. This picturesque area of the national seashore has a scenic beach, but getting to it is difficult. The journey starts with Bound Brook Island Road off Rt. 6. It is unpaved and uneven, so it might be better to park and walk or bike to it if you do not have a four-wheel-drive vehicle. The surface of the road is a few feet below grade, making it feel like you are driving down a chute. There are very few places to turn around until the small beach parking lot.

BOUND BROOK ISLAND

Once you make it to the beach, though, your effort will seem worthwhile. There is a sandy pathway leading over the dunes to a beach with a broad view across Cape Cod Bay. On a clear day it is possible to see straight across to Plymouth and other South Shore communities. While the view from the shore is amazing, the best view of all is from a sloping, sandy hill near the beach at the end of Bound Brook Island Road. A path leads to its summit, which is more than 70 feet high. From there you will feel as though you can see from Provincetown to Maine. This view by itself makes the tough trek to the beach a mere footnote. The large dune is not a climb for everyone, but the view from the sandy pathway to the beach is nearly as good for those who do not wish to attempt the dune.

Important Info:
- Limited free parking
- No lifeguard
- No concessions
- Dogs allowed October 16 to May 31

SUNSET AT BOUND BROOK ISLAND

IX
TRURO

1. Pine Grove Cemetery

For travelers who crave the darker side of Cape Cod, this place will easily suffice. Pine Grove Cemetery, remotely located more than a half mile from any homes, is the scene of perhaps the most-horrific crimes ever committed on Cape Cod: the Antone Costa Murders.

The murders occurred in 1968 and included mutilation and dismemberment of several young girls' bodies. The murderer was Antone Costa, who became the subject of a book titled *In His Garden*, written by Leo Damore. Costa died in his prison cell in 1974, purportedly by hanging himself.

The cemetery was the subject of paranormal research in 2007, with a few odd occurrences happening to the investigating team, although nothing overwhelming. The most interesting area they encountered was a small 8-by-8-foot crypt at the rear of the cemetery. The crypt was once used to house bodies during winter, when the ground was too cold for them to be buried. It was in the woods near the back of the cemetery where Costa seemingly mutilated and buried his victims' bodies.

When I visited the cemetery at dusk on a misty, foggy afternoon, I spent some time inside the crypt (which is now chained shut). Mysteriously, my cell phone battery died in an instant, which I am told was due to a spirit using surrounding energy to manifest itself.

Even if you are not daring enough to wander the grounds where such terrifying crimes took place, the cemetery is a historical footnote, and a quick drive by the crypt can't hurt . . . can it?

Important Info:
• Parking is free

THE CRYPT AT PINE GROVE CEMETERY

PINE GROVE CEMETERY

Pine Grove Cemetery
Truro

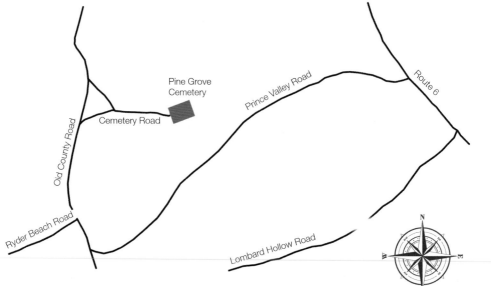

2. Pamet Harbor

Pamet Harbor is considered one of the birthplaces of the American whaling industry. The harbor is named for the tribe of Native Americans that inhabited the land at the time of the arrival of the first European settlers. Near the end of the Pilgrims' voyage, there was a stopover in what is now Truro. The Pilgrims and the Pamet tribe fired upon one another, but nobody was killed. Soon after, the Pilgrims sailed off and landed in Plymouth.

The land was purchased from the Pamet tribe in 1689 and became known as Truro in 1709. Known for farming until the early nineteenth century, whaling soon became a central part of life. The harbor and the whaling industry in Truro boomed until a great storm destroyed the fishing fleet in 1841. After a brief revival that lasted into the 1860s, the town quieted down and remains a quaint village to this day.

Truro's harbor has beautiful scenery, including the Pamet River, Pamet Marsh, and the beach area. The Pamet Harbor Yacht & Tennis Club, adjacent to the harbor, should be visited during a trip to Truro.

Important Info:
- Parking is free
- No lifeguards
- No concessions
- $20 fee for boat launch

PAMET HARBOR

GPS: (41.99924698146824, -70.0212559086888)
Address: South Pamet Road, Truro

3. Ballston Beach

This ocean-side beach stretches out in the shadows of the high Truro bluffs. It has seen its share of changes from erosion, including a storm that pushed sand back several hundred yards into the Pamet River. This change gives it a unique look. From here it is possible to walk uninterrupted all the way north to Race Point in Provincetown, or south to Coast Guard Beach in Eastham. It is a residents' beach during the summer season, so keep that in mind when timing a visit to this beautifully remote spot.

Important Info:
• Parking: residents only mid-June through Labor Day

A HOME ON THE EDGE
OF THE BLUFFS AT
BALLSTON BEACH

BALLSTON BEACH IN
TRURO

4. Bearberry Hill

The east summit of this spot reaches about 60 feet above sea level. It is high enough to give a sprawling view of the surrounding area, including Ballston Beach below. Across the road from the summit of the hill is also the HI Truro Hostel. For decades this building was a right of passage for local children, who could spend a week here for school learning about Cape Cod ecology through the national seashore. The Pamet Area trails bring you either out to the beach or to the unique Bog House. It is unique for the fact that its front door is on the second floor. It was originally one floor but was raised to create storage below for harvesting cranberries.

Important Info:
• Parking: limited along the roadside

THE BOG HOUSE IN TRURO

SUNSET AT BEARBERRY HILL IN TRURO

5. Cape Cod or Highland Lighthouse

Highland Light, which is surrounded by the Highland Links Golf Course, is the oldest lighthouse on Cape Cod. The first Highland Lighthouse was built in 1797. The current tower was finished in 1857 and is the third lighthouse built near this site. In 1996, when erosion brought it to less than 100 feet from the edge of the 120-foot-high cliff, the current lighthouse was moved back 453 feet to save it from possible collapse.

The lighthouse has two names. The National Oceanic and Atmospheric Administration (NOAA) lists the lighthouse as Cape Cod Light, while locals

HIGHLAND LIGHTHOUSE

know it as Highland Light because it resides in the "highlands" of Truro. From the lighthouse looking south, one can see several structures that are on the grounds of the defunct North Truro Air Force Station. Although it is no longer operational, this is considered government property and cannot be explored.

A stone marks the spot where the lighthouse sat until its move in 1996. Today the stone is less than 100 feet from the edge of the bluff, which confirms just how necessary the move was. The lighthouse is owned by the national seashore and managed by the nonprofit group Highland Museum and Light, Inc. Views of the shore below and across to Provincetown are amazing and should be experienced by every visitor to Cape Cod. It underwent an extensive renovation in 2021.

Important Info:
- Parking is free
- Concessions at Highland Links Snack Bar
- Tours of lighthouse mid-May to mid-October
- Admission: $6 for adults and $5 for students and seniors

HIGHLAND HOUSE, TRURO

GPS: Montano's Restaurant (42.044966, -70.095827)
Gravesite (42.051332, -70.093483) (*this is an approximation*)
Address: 481 Route 6, North Truro

6. The Grave of Thomas Ridley
North Truro

Thousands of people pass by Montano's Restaurant on Rt. 6 in North Truro every year, but it is what lies deep in the woods behind Montano's that is of interest here . . . if you can find it: the grave of Thomas Ridley. Thomas Ridley died of smallpox in 1776. He was a fisherman who had ten children with his wife, Elizabeth. After he died, his body was taken deep into the North Truro woods and buried far from civilization for fear of the deadly disease spreading. His wife lived to be seventy-four and was buried in Provincetown Cemetery Number 1.

Montano's Restaurant is the jumping-off point for this adventure, but only a handful of people, including myself, have ever successfully found this grave. It is barely more than a foot tall and a foot wide and is surrounded by trees, brush, and debris, masking it almost entirely from anyone not right on top of it. Directions leading to the stone itself are difficult to give. There is a sand pit a few hundred feet behind Montano's, to the northeast. It is said that if you find the sand pit, you have a fighting chance to find the grave.

From the sand pit, take a right turn following an overgrown fire road. In these woods there are many kettle holes left by receding glaciers; it is the second kettle hole on the left that you are meant to circumnavigate. Go around the right of this kettle hole and between two others, where you go left. As you head back toward the beginning, you should nearly trip over the grave. It is hardly an easy task.

The truly adventurous should definitely try their hand at finding a place that so few have ever seen or even know about. Just beware it is easy to get lost in these woods. Also remember after a long hike through the woods to stop in Montano's for some delicious Italian cuisine.

Important Info:
• Parking at Montano's Restaurant is free

MONTANO'S
RESTAURANT,
N. TRURO

THE PATHWAY TO THE SECRET GRAVE
OF THOMAS RIDLEY

THE GRAVE OF THOMAS RIDLEY

7. Pilgrim Lake
North Truro

This is an area that hundreds of thousands of people pass by each year, but only a very few stop to see the lake. It is named for the Pilgrims who skirted along the shores here, on their way across to Corn Hill. In the seventeenth century the lake was a harbor.

Pilgrim Lake is on the eastern side of Rt. 6, just before Provincetown. It is bordered by huge sand dunes and is part of the national seashore. The lake looks impressive, even when passing it by at more than 50 miles per hour. However, a quick turn onto High Head Road leads to one of the most breathtaking views on the entire Cape.

High Head Road quickly goes uphill, leading to several places that overlook the lake. In 2004 the tidal flow was restored to Pilgrim Lake, thanks to a man-made culvert connecting it to the eastern side of Provincetown Harbor. There is a dirt parking area at the base of the hill on High Head Road, where a walking trail takes you around some of the lake area. Hiking is a good option, but the views from up above, on High Head Road, are most impressive. There are also picturesque views of Pilgrim Lake a short drive south at Pilgrim Heights, along a walk on the Pilgrim Springs Trail.

Important Info:
- Parking is free
- No lifeguard
- No concessions

PILGRIM LAKE

X

PROVINCETOWN

GPS: (42.06616668619918, -70.16287629052889)
Address: Snail Road / Route 6, Provincetown

1. Province Lands Dune Shacks

There are nineteen rustic shacks that reside in the dunes of Provincetown. They are a part of the Peaked Hill Bars Historic District. Many of the shacks date back more than a century and have been passed down through generations. It is possible to park and walk nearly a mile over soft, rolling sand dunes to view these pieces of history. Famed artists such as Tennessee Williams, Jack Kerouac, E.E. Cummings, and Jackson Pollock made these shacks home for a period of creativity.

It is important to remember that these are privately owned and to keep a respectful distance, especially when they are occupied. A few of them are available to be rented if one wishes to turn back the clock to the early twentieth century. Art's Dune Tours provides a safe way to venture out among the natural beauty of the Province Lands area.

AMONG THE
PEAKED HILL BARS
DUNE SHACKS IN
PROVINCETOWN

AMONG THE
PEAKED HILL BARS
DUNE SHACKS IN
PROVINCETOWN

2. Race Point Lighthouse

This amazing area can be accessed one of two ways: from Race Point Beach or from Herring Cove Beach. The easier route is from Herring Cove Beach, where the Province Lands Bike Trail begins. Race Point Lighthouse, built in 1876, sits roughly a mile and a half from the Herring Cove Beach parking lot, and the view is worth the walk.

The paved bike trail that winds through the tall sand dunes is like a different world. A very scenic dirt road that forks off toward the lighthouse on the left features a beautiful marsh on the left and Provincetown Municipal Airport on the right. Small planes occasionally pass overhead, breaking the otherwise quiet atmosphere.

It is faster to drive to the lighthouse, but an off-road permit is required. Besides, standing before Race Point Lighthouse after completing the full walk is even more satisfying. This is the tip of the Cape, with the entirety of it stretching out behind you. From May through October the lighthouse keeper's house, as well as the beautifully renovated brick Whistle House, are available for rent by the day or week.

RACE POINT LIGHTHOUSE

With nothing but the sound of the ocean waves crashing all around, it is easy to lose track of time while standing in the shadow of Race Point Light, and that is not a bad thing. The name "Race Point" refers to the strong crosscurrents that occur here at the very top of the arm of Cape Cod.

Important Info:
- Parking along Province Lands Road is free. There is also parking at Herring Cove Beach: daily fee, $25.
- Lifeguard and concessions in season
- Province Lands Road parking GPS (42.061861, -70.217262)

THE LIGHTHOUSE
KEEPER'S HOUSE

THE VIEW OF RACE
POINT LIGHTHOUSE
FROM ACROSS THE
MARSH

OLD HARBOR LIFE-SAVING
STATION AT RACE POINT

NATIONAL PARK SERVICE
BUILDING AT RACE POINT

3. Province Lands Bike Path

Not as long or as well known as the main stretch of the Cape Cod Rail Trail, this 7.5-mile bike path has some of the most beautiful, unspoiled scenery one could hope to see on Cape Cod. Beginning at Herring Cove Beach, the path includes several offshoots. Elusive Race Point Light is down a dirt road adjacent to the path and is a worthwhile walk. Plus, there are many views of the nearby Pilgrim Monument, which towers above the dunes and pine trees. Some of the sand dunes rise 20 to 30 feet into the air, adding to the splendor of the ride and giving the bike path a secluded feel.

The path ends at Race Point Beach, the northernmost point on the Cape, which should be explored if time permits. You do not need to ride a bicycle; this is an amazing place to walk or run as well. Though much of the trails are sand, there are some spots with tree cover, including the beech forest. It is possible to see a traditional cranberry bog among the 4,000 acres of the Province Lands area. In 2009 the path was improved, including widening and resurfacing 2.5 miles of the asphalt. This has made the experience even better for all riders, runners, and walkers.

Important Info:
• Parking is at Herring Cove Beach. Daily parking $25.
• Lifeguard and concessions in season

PROVINCE LANDS BIKE PATH

GPS: Wood End Light (42.021245, -70.193504)
Long Point Light (42.033138, -70.168627)
Address: West end of Commercial Street, Provincetown

4. Wood End Lighthouse

Though not quite as difficult to reach as Race Point Light, getting to Wood End Lighthouse is an exercise in determination if it is to be seen up close. Parking can be at a premium at the beginning of Province Lands Road, so that is the first step to accomplish. The next step is a walk across the nearly mile-long breakwater that stretches across the western edge of Provincetown Harbor. The breakwater is fairly level, but the distance discourages people. The journey to the lighthouse is one to remember. About halfway across the breakwater, turn around and take a look at the spectacular Pilgrim Monument looming high above the rest of Provincetown.

Built in 1872, Wood End Lighthouse sits stoically among the small dunes and beach grasses. As at Race Point Light, standing before the white stone rectangle is quiet and peaceful. At 39 feet tall it is hard to miss from the street, and if you turn to the left there is another white rectangle farther down the beach: Long Point Lighthouse.

WOOD END LIGHTHOUSE

5. Long Point Lighthouse

Located a little more than a mile and a half from Wood End Lighthouse, this nearly identical light station was built shortly after a settlement was formed in 1818. At its peak the settlement held nearly two hundred people. Some of the houses built during the time of that settlement were floated from the end of Long Point across to Provincetown's West End; they are designated by plaques.

From the tip of Long Point there is a clear view across Provincetown Harbor to where Rt. 6 and Rt. 6A come up from the south. You can also make out a few of the collections of identical cottages that line the water in North Truro.

This may be one of the most isolated lighthouses on the Cape, and very few people have the desire to walk a mile along a breakwater and then another mile and a half on sand to reach it. Once there, it is as if you are alone in the world.

There is a small dune next to the lighthouse with a wooden cross on top. The cross is adorned with a tattered American flag and a nameplate that reads: "Charles S. Darby: 'Gallant Soldier,' Killed In Action Oct. 17, 1944."

Long Point Lighthouse is a place that many have seen but few have been in its shadow. Give it a try.

Important Info:
• There is free but limited parking at the end of Commercial Street

LONG POINT LIGHTHOUSE

THE WOODEN CROSS NEAR LONG POINT LIGHTHOUSE

GPS: (42.04291331239655, -70.1928376502512)

Address: 73 Commercial Street, Provincetown

6. Captain Jack's Wharf

These consist of a beautifully eclectic and rustic collection of Cape Cod cabins on a wharf over Provincetown Harbor. Each of the cabins is available for rent from Memorial Day weekend through mid-October. The wharf itself was built in 1897 by Jackson Williams, a.k.a. Captain Jack. Each of the fifteen cabins has a unique name, including Ribbons, where legendary playwright Tennessee Williams is said to have worked on his iconic *Street Car* and *Glass Menagerie*. Other cabins have fantastic names such as Nautilus, Borealis, Jupiter, and more. Even if not looking for a getaway stay, it is still a fun and historic location to be around.

CAPTAIN JACK'S WHARF IN PROVINCETOWN

7. Pilgrim Monument

Standing 252 feet high and perched atop High Pole Hill, the point of Pilgrim Monument is 350 feet above sea level, making it a prime destination. It commemorates the Pilgrims' first landing place on their journey from England to America in 1620. The Pilgrims spent five weeks exploring the tip of the Cape before heading across the bay to Plymouth. While they were here, on November 11, 1620, they signed the Mayflower Compact, which was the first document of the democratic society in the New World and the original governing document of Plymouth Colony.

PILGRIM MONUMENT

The inside of the monument is unique. Etched in some of the granite blocks on the climb are the names of many towns across the United States that donated stones for the monument. The cornerstone was laid in 1907 by President Theodore Roosevelt, and the tower was dedicated by President Taft three years later. It celebrated its one hundredth anniversary in 2010.

From the top the view is nothing short of spectacular. All of Provincetown is clearly visible, as is the national seashore area leading down the "arm" of the Cape toward Orleans and Brewster. On a clear day it is possible to see across Cape Cod Bay toward the South Shore, Plymouth, and Boston. The sixty ramps and 116 steps it takes to climb the monument should not deter anybody from enjoying this landmark.

In time for the 2022 season, a new inclined elevator opened. This allows people to access the museum and monument from Bradford Street.

Important Info:
- Parking is free for 2 hours with paid admission
- Admission: Adult (18–64), $20.94; Teen (13–17) and Seniors (65+), $16.75; children (4–12), $9.42; children 3 & under, free

VIEWS OF PROVINCETOWN FROM THE TOP OF THE PILGRIM MONUMENT

GPS: (42.05526503421769, -70.19358330442981)
Address: Jerome Smith Road, Provincetown

8. St. Peter's Cemetery

This place is both fascinating and somber. It is here that two of Cape Cod's most notorious crimes intersect. Both Tony Costa and the Lady of the Dunes have their final resting places among the thousands of graves here. Tony Costa's grave is unmarked, while the Lady of the Dunes in October 2022 was at long last identified as Ruth Marie Terry and has a new stone. Her grave can be found to the right of the chapel at the bottom of the hill and is routinely covered in beautiful trinkets in her memory.

THE ENTRANCE TO ST. PETER'S CEMETERY IN PROVINCETOWN

THE GRAVE OF THE LADY OF THE DUNES AT ST. PETER'S

XI

CHATHAM

1. Chatham Bars Inn

The epitome of luxury inside, with the most beautiful of views on the outside. It is easy to see why this is one of the icons of Cape Cod lodging and has been for more than a century. Charles Ashley Hardy built this establishment in 1914, originally as a semiprivate hunting lodge. Today it is a world-class luxury resort with 217 rooms, an off-site farm, spa, private beach, and four restaurants. CBI is open to the public for dining, with rooms at a premium even in winter. It is also a highly popular location for destination weddings.

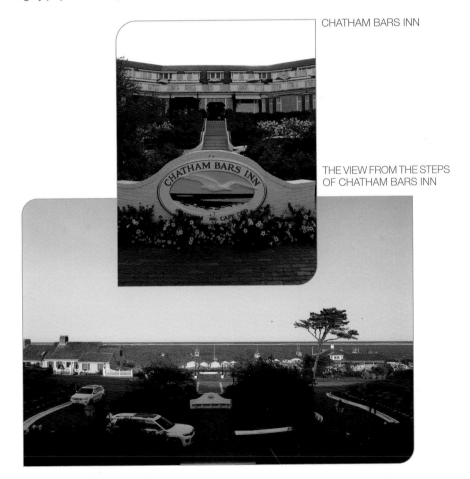

CHATHAM BARS INN

THE VIEW FROM THE STEPS OF CHATHAM BARS INN

2. Chatham Lighthouse

A part of the Coast Guard station, Chatham Lighthouse was originally built in 1877, but the station itself was established in 1808 under orders from President Thomas Jefferson. For 115 years the Chatham Light station consisted of two lighthouses. In 1923 one of the lights was moved to Eastham, where it became Nauset Light. The remaining light stands majestically overlooking North Beach, and the view from the sand looking up at the lighthouse is spectacular.

The original Chatham Light lantern and lens were removed in 1969 and are currently on display at the historic Atwood House, a short drive away on Stage Harbor Road. The lighthouse is not open to the public except for special tours during the warmer months, but the view of this Cape landmark is spectacular from just beyond the fence as well.

Important Info:
• Free 30-minute parking across the street (strictly enforced)

CHATHAM LIGHTHOUSE

3. North Beach Island

North Beach is near the end of Main Street in Chatham, directly across from Chatham Lighthouse, and is a continuation of Nauset Beach in Orleans. The beaches can be observed easily from the elevated parking lot, which also has three sets of powerful binoculars to aid viewing.

The story of the formation and destruction of this beach is every bit as interesting as any Cape Cod story. Up until 1987 the beach had been known as a "barrier beach" and continued down toward Monomoy Island. Then a huge winter storm caused a break in the beach directly opposite Chatham Light, which eventually widened and caused the loss of seven North Beach cottages. A second break occurred in 2007 a little farther north, and the initial break has now widened to nearly 2 miles. In recent years the island has been growing again due to loss of sand at Nauset Beach. This is a fascinating story of the ocean versus the land.

The beach is quite popular during the summer, with the inner harbor area known as Lighthouse Beach being frequently packed with people and caused by the break in the beach being used as a starting point for windsurfers. Even though there has been much change to North Beach Island, it is still a large and popular recreational area. It is located roughly 20 feet below the surface of the road, which is why the views looking down on the beach are so unusual.

Important Info:
- Free 30-minute parking, otherwise a current beach sticker is required ($50 citation if not)
- No lifeguard
- No concessions
- Dogs allowed Labor Day–Memorial Day

NORTH BEACH

SUNRISE AT NORTH BEACH

4. Monomoy National Wildlife Refuge

A short drive from Chatham Light down Morris Island Road, this 7,600-acre wildlife sanctuary is filled with natural beauty perfect for sightseeing and school field trips. It is a great spot to spend the day with the family. Even the drive out to the wildlife refuge is filled with beautiful scenery. Monomoy is the only designated wilderness area in southern New England; most of the acreage was set aside as such in 1970. The name "Monomoy" is believed to come from the Algonquin tribe's word "munumuhkemoo," meaning "there is a rushing of mighty water."

Visitors will find a trail that leads along the high cliffs and has a great view of the northern portion of Monomoy Island. There is a weather radar station behind a fence along the trail as well. Unfortunately, in 2021 severe erosion caused the need for the removal of a set of stairs that led down to the beach. To walk the beach at low tide, one must access the beach farther north.

Once you start to walk south, there is complete solitude, except for the occasional passing of small fishing boats into the harbor. It is a very relaxing walk, as the rushing waves and salty breezes melt away any conscious thoughts. The walk along the beach ends with a panoramic view of Monomoy Island, which, at low tide, sits only a few hundred feet offshore. The remainder of the walk leads west to Stage Harbor Lighthouse, across the mouth of the harbor.

Monomoy Island can be accessed by boat; the lighthouse is on the southern half of the island. This is the only reminder of any past human habitation on Monomoy. There are daily excursions to Monomoy for seal watching or to take a walk on the island.

Important Info:
• Parking is free

MONOMOY WILDLIFE
REFUGE, CHATHAM

5. Atwood House Museum

The Atwood House, which is now a museum and the centerpiece of the Chatham Historical Society, is virtually unchanged since it was built by sea captain Joseph Atwood in 1752. Five generations of the Atwood family were raised in the house. The only major change in the historic home is the wing added to it in 1833 by Joseph Atwood's grandson, John, for his wife.

In addition to the Atwood House there are other things to see on the grounds. The museum has nearly 3,000 items of art, decorative arts, maritime artifacts, and more related to Chatham history, many of them on display.

The Nickerson North Beach Camp—also on the grounds—was built in 1947 by Joshua Atkins Nickerson II, a descendent of Chatham founder William Nickerson. Prior to being moved to the museum complex in 1991, it was part of a row of about fifty similar dune shacks found along North Beach before the break in the beach in 1987. In the years right after World War II, you could lug your own materials to the beach and build a dune shack.

On the far side of the parking lot is one of the original lanterns of the Chatham Twin Lights. The Twin Lights consisted of Chatham Light, still standing overlooking North Beach, and a second light that became Nauset Light when it was moved to Eastham in 1923. The lantern was removed from Chatham Light in 1969 and donated to the Historical Society. With the lantern intact, it is possible to walk around on it and imagine what it was like when this piece of history was guiding ships that came close to North Beach more than sixty years ago.

Important Info:
• Admission: adults, $10; students (8–17), $5; children (7 and under) and members are free

ATWOOD HOUSE MUSEUM

NICKERSON NORTH BEACH CAMP

ONE OF THE OLD CHATHAM LIGHTHOUSE LANTERNS

6. Godfrey Windmill

Originally built in 1797 by Col. Benjamin Godfrey, this wooden windmill is on Rink Hill as a part of Chase Park. It originally sat on the east side of Stage Harbor Road before being moved to its current spot in 1955, after being donated to the town by the Crocker family. It is one of the last surviving wooden windmills in Massachusetts and one of only seven windmills on Cape Cod that are open to the public. The structure was fully restored in 2012. It is routinely open to the public during the summer.

Also on the grounds is the wonderfully unusual Chatham Labyrinth. It is an exact replica of the eleven-circuit medieval labyrinth found in the floor of the Chartres Cathedral in France.

GODFREY WINDMILL AT CHASE PARK IN CHATHAM

THE CHATHAM LABYRINTH AT CHASE PARK

7. Stage Harbor Lighthouse

Finding this semihidden lighthouse can be another worthwhile Cape Cod hike. To visit it, you need to take a trip to Harding's Beach, which has two parking lots connected by a short road and a fabulous view of Monomoy Island to the east.

Stage Harbor Light is visible from the moment you arrive at the second parking lot, though it is about a mile down the beach. The tower was built in 1880, but the light was deactivated in 1933. The lantern has been removed and the surrounding property is private, but you can get a close look while respecting the boundaries. The removal of the lantern gave the structure an odd appearance, but it is absolutely a lighthouse.

The pathway to the light is used by vehicles, and the walk is much easier than places such as Race Point, Wood End, and Long Point Lights. Along with the skeleton of the lighthouse, the original lighthouse keeper's house, a shed, and an outhouse remain on the property. Once you reach the mouth of Stage Harbor, where the lighthouse stands, you should allow time to sit on the sand and enjoy the sounds of the waves. It is a popular area to fish and to watch boats entering and leaving the harbor.

Important Info:
- Parking at Hardings Beach; daily fee, $20
- Lifeguards and concessions in season
- Dogs allowed Labor Day–Memorial Day

HARDING'S BEACH

STAGE HARBOR LIGHTHOUSE

8. Forest Beach, the Second Marconi Site

Forest Beach is another in a string of beautiful south-facing beaches on Cape Cod. It is a stretch of sand perfect for walking, with great views of Monomoy Island and Stage Harbor Lighthouse. There are also trails that lead you to nearby Cockle Cove.

It might surprise a lot of visitors and perhaps some locals to find out the historical significance of Forest Beach. Behind the beach, in the marshy area, there are four cement pillars in a square pattern that represent the remains of a WCC radio tower used by the Marines. The WCC station was owned by RCA, which bought the equipment from Guglielmo Marconi's company in 1920. The tower, erected in 1948, once stood 300 feet high, overlooking the water, and remained there until the land was bought by the town. It is considered by some to be a second Marconi site, though he was not directly involved with it. Not as well known or as directly connected to Marconi as the site in Wellfleet, this site is still historic. The Forest Beach overlook behind the marsh area has a plaque with the historical details.

Important Info:
- Parking is free, but the lot is small; first come, first serve
- No lifeguard
- No concessions
- Dogs allowed Labor Day–Memorial Day

HOW THE RADIO TOWER LOOKED

THE RADIO TOWER
BASE AT FOREST
STREET BEACH

FOREST STREET BEACH

VIEW FROM THE FOREST
BEACH OVERLOOK

XII

HARWICH

1. Wequassett Resort and Golf Club

A five-star luxury resort that is deserving of all of its praise, Wequassett is a destination for locals and visitors far and wide. Twenty-two buildings make up the resort, including five highly rated restaurants and the Eben Ryder House, commonly known as "Square Top." It was begun modestly in 1925 by Carroll Nickerson and his wife, Emogen, with only an oilcloth sign and word of mouth for advertising. Today it is Cape Cod's only five-star resort according to *Forbes Travel Guide*, having first achieved the distinction in 2016. One trip to Wequassett will show why it is one of only 199 five-star resorts in the world.

EVENING AT WEQUASSETT RESORT

2. Red River Beach

Harwich Port

The largest beach in Harwich is accessible from three different roads. The Red River, which lies at the eastern end of the long parking lot, marks the border between Harwich and Chatham. From the eastern end of the parking lot, there are amazing views of Chatham, Monomoy Island, and Red River. A jetty sticks out 40 feet or so into the water, where one can take in all of the breathtaking Cape Cod scenery.

The beach stretches between Red River and Wychmere Harbor. The Wychmere Harbor Club stands stoically at the west end of the beach, just across the opening to the harbor. The east end of the parking lot is popular with boaters and kayakers taking short trips across Nantucket Sound to Monomoy Island.

Important Info:
- Daily parking, $20
- Lifeguards in season
- Dogs allowed Labor Day–Memorial Day

RED RIVER BEACH

GPS: (41.66844, -70.0662)
Address: Route 28, Harwich Port

3. Wychmere Harbor
Harwich Port

A well-known spot in Harwich, this beautiful man-made harbor can be seen from Rt. 28. It is a spectacular sight, since the harbor is downhill from the road, giving one a chance to experience a panoramic view of boats and the ocean. Luckily, on Rt. 28 there is a small dirt turnoff at the top of the hill, on Rt. 28, that affords any passersby the opportunity to stop and take a longer, safer look at Wychmere Harbor. On many warm summer days, you may see several people stopped to take photographs, to paint the harbor scene, or simply sitting to take in the scenery.

On the east side of the harbor is Harbor Road, which leads to a marina where people leave their boats during the warmer months. Here visitors can get closer looks at many vessels, small and large. On the opposite side, sitting on Snow Inn Road, is the Wychmere Beach Club. This popular spot housed Thompson's Clam Bar, a famous Cape Cod landmark, until it closed in 1995. The Beach Club has now come into its own as a beautiful spot for weddings and other outdoor events, thanks to its location on 14 acres of prime beachfront land.

Important Info:
• Very limited free parking on Rt. 28

WYCHMERE HARBOR

4. Old Colony Rail Trail

An offshoot of the main Cape Cod Rail Trail, this 7.5-mile extension takes a rider, walker, or runner from Harwich into Chatham. Named the Old Colony Rail Trail, it honors the abandoned railroad line that the path traces.

This extension of the Rail Trail begins at a rotary in Harwich and ends at Crowell Road in Chatham. It was opened in 2005 and allows you to get acquainted with another section of Cape Cod. Here you will see several ponds, a horse farm, and eventually Chatham Airport. From the end of the rail trail extension, it is a very short trip into the center of Chatham. There is also a "Chatham Loop," which is an extra mile of trail that brings you out to Chatham Lighthouse.

One does not have to travel the entire length, since there are several parking areas along the way for those who wish to cover only a segment of the trail.

Important Info:

• Free parking is available behind the First Congregational Church on Rt. 124

THE ROTARY AT THE BEGINNING OF THE OLD COLONY RAIL TRAIL

Old Colony Rail Trail
Harwich

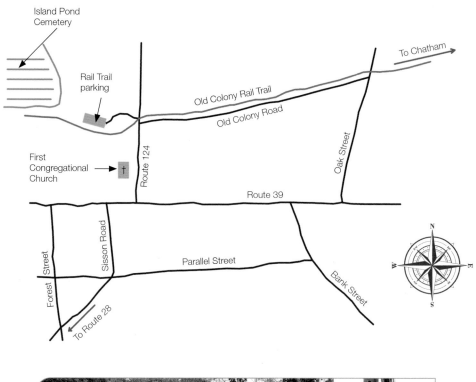

THE OLD COLONY RAIL TRAIL HEADING TOWARD CHATHAM

GPS: (41.687792, -70.115574)
Address: Bells Neck Road, West Harwich

5. Bells Neck Conservation Area

There are many conservation areas on Cape Cod, some large, some small. At more than 250 acres of natural beauty, Bells Neck is a large conservation area, but it is not very well known outside the local area. It has walking trails, ponds, and an amazing marsh that includes a view of an immense blue water tower hovering above the treeline. There are several entrances to this area; the most widely used is the Great Western Road entrance to Bells Neck Road. Entering this way, you will see the large West Reservoir on the right side. It is nearly always populated by swans and ducks during the warmer months. There is a chance you might even see a majestic bald eagle. A main dirt road with several side roads leads to other trails and secluded spots for hiking or enjoying a quiet lunch.

Bells Neck Road continues to Route 28, but there is one side road that should be taken. N Road takes you to the marsh area at Bells Neck and a walking bridge that gives an amazing perspective. The conservation area is in full view from this spot. The muddy area along the marsh river is filled with tiny marsh fiddler crabs that scurry away as you approach.

All the trails are great for walking, and the Cape Cod Rail Trail slices through the conservation area as it makes its way from Dennis to Wellfleet. This short detour gives travelers a quick view of Bells Neck.

Important Info:
• Free parking

A CLOUDY DAY VIEW
OF BELLS NECK

XIII

WEST DENNIS
& SOUTH DENNIS

GPS: (41.690067, -70.151473)
Address: Rt. 134, Wellfleet

1. Cape Cod Rail Trail

The longest of the three recreational paths on Cape Cod, the Cape Cod Rail Trail (CCRT) is a way to absorb the soul of the Cape. At more than 20 miles in length, spanning from Dennis to Wellfleet, the CCRT combines a little of everything that makes Cape Cod beautiful. Many smaller parking areas along the route give even a novice rider or runner access to the Rail Trail without needing to start at the beginning. In 2016 the Rail Trail was extended west into Yarmouth, with eventual hopes to extend into Hyannis.

The trail winds through the Bells Neck Conservation area in Harwich, over the highway, and past a cranberry bog before sliding past the Pleasant Lake General Store, which is a perfect spot to rest and grab something to drink. There are a few ponds along the route for taking a dip on a hot day, but the trail is somewhat shaded, which does help keep one cooler.

As discussed earlier, the CCRT breaks off near Chatham and also passes through Nickerson State Park, which has its own separate bike path. Once the CCRT passes over the highway again, it begins its ascent into the national seashore, which can be seen on a bike or on foot. From the trail one can observe Herring Pond, Depot Pond, and Great Pond in Eastham. The Marconi Station site is also on the way in Wellfleet, though it is a bit off the trail.

The main artery of the Cape Cod Rail Trail currently ends at Lecount Hollow Road in Wellfleet, where there is a parking area for those wishing to follow the trail in reverse (the trail is being extended a few miles farther, though, as of 2022). Whether you are a novice rider or runner, or an expert, or just want a pleasant nature stroll, the CCRT can be enjoyed by anyone, at any point, and at just about any time.

Important Info:
- Free parking at beginning of bike path
- Concessions at beginning of bike path in season

THE PLEASANT LAKE GENERAL STORE ALONG THE CAPE COD RAIL TRAIL

THE CAPE COD RAIL TRAIL HEADING UP TOWARD THE NATIONAL SEASHORE

2. Indian Lands Conservation Area

Located along the Cape Cod Rail Trail, the Indian Lands Conservation Area includes a set of paths that lead down toward Bass River, with a great view of Highbank Bridge. The master path runs along the power lines and is a tougher hike, with soft sand and stones. The other path was once railroad tracks but is now part of the larger rail trail. There is currently a plan to extend the Cape Cod Rail Trail from Dennis through to Barnstable, and the railroad tracks are the route for the new extension. People park at the nearby highway rest area to fish from the banks of the river.

Abutting the parking lot is another piece of history called either Old South Dennis Cemetery or Dennis Ancient Cemetery. It lies behind the town offices in a fenced-in area but is accessible. The gravestones bear some of the names long associated with Cape Cod, such as Baker, Bangs, and Nickerson. Walking past these stones is like a crash course in Cape Cod history, reminding visitors and residents alike of who came before them.

Important Info:
• Free parking

THE ENTRANCE TO THE SOUTH DENNIS CEMETERY

THE ENTRANCE TO THE INDIAN TRAILS

BASS RIVER ALONG THE INDIAN TRAILS

GPS: (41.651238, -70.175797)
Address: Davis Beach Road, West Dennis

3. West Dennis Beach

With nearly a mile and a half of pristine sand between Bass River and the neighboring Lighthouse Inn, West Dennis Beach is a very popular south-facing beach in the Mid-Cape area. The long parking lot is perfect for walking or running, and there is even an area designated for kitesurfing. The jetty that stretches into the water at the west end of the beach is used for fishing but also gives one a great view of Bass River and across the water to Smuggler's Beach. About a mile off shore is a small rock cluster used as a destination for boaters or swimmers

THE MOUTH OF BASS RIVER FROM WEST DENNIS BEACH.

to relax away from the crowds. Before beginning an excursion out to it, remember that it looks closer than it is.

At the eastern end of the beach, a smaller parking area gives access to a new series of man-made sand dunes, built, complete with beach grass and fences, to protect the beach from the ravages of erosion and help replenish it. For those visiting for the first time, the "new" sand dunes will appear as a natural part of the environment.

On the north side of the parking lot, a marsh has many beautiful homes located across it. When the tide rises, there are many perfect photo opportunities, with the calm water acting as a mirror. The marsh water eventually runs farther east and empties into Uncle Stephans Pond, located among more summer homes and rentals. Despite the size of the parking area, West Dennis Beac

is packed on most summer days, so it is wise to arrive early—which gives you more time to enjoy this amazing beach.

Important Info:

- Daily parking, $30
- Lifeguards and concessions in season
- Dogs allowed Labor Day–Memorial Day

SUNSET AT WEST DENNIS BEACH

XIV

YARMOUTH

GPS: (41.684776392536534, -70.1605205430705)
Address: 440 Highbank Road, South Yarmouth

1. Wilbur Park

This small beach on Bass River is known more for fishing and boating than swimming, but swimming is still a big part of it. The land that makes up the park was donated to the town in 1956 by Dr. George Wilbur and his wife, Barbara. Wilbur also donated land across the river in Dennis along Cove Road for a town landing. The park has been routinely improved over the decades, making it a lesser-known treasure in the town.

Important Info:
• Free parking

GPS: (41.670336, -70.191444)
Address: Indian Memorial Drive, South Yarmouth

2. Indian Memorial
South Yarmouth

A simple memorial of carefully placed stones on the side of Indian Memorial Drive is a sacred place in Cape Cod history, although it seems unassuming to most. Near the memorial there was once a Native American cemetery situated close to Long Pond. Native Americans were buried on land owned by Robert Howes that was subsequently proposed to be used for a saltworks. Their bodies were exhumed and reburied, and later this monument was raised to mark the site of the original cemetery.

INDIAN MEMORIAL

Now a quiet residential street, this is not as well known as some other Native American burial plots. Its story and historical significance deserve to be shared, and the memorial should be visited.

Important Info:
• No parking area at the memorial, but a single car can pull off the road. Parking available at nearby Long Pond Beach, daily rate $20.

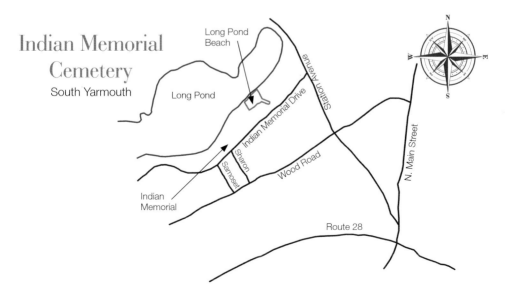

Indian Memorial Cemetery
South Yarmouth

Long Pond Beach

Long Pond

Station Avenue

Indian Memorial Drive

N. Main Street

Sharon

Samoset

Wood Road

Indian Memorial

Route 28

GPS: (41.65652716216276, -70.19715430743233)
Address: River Street / Pleasant Street, South Yarmouth

3. America's First Traffic Circle

On a quiet area of the Bass River Historic District sits an unassuming piece of American history. The very first traffic circle, or rotary, sits at the meeting of Pleasant and River Streets. Originally an old watering trough, it was transformed into a traffic circle in the first decade of the twentieth century by Charles Henry Davis. It was called National Highways Circle, paying homage to Davis's role in the National Highways Association. The traffic circle stands much as it did more than a century ago, minus the three ship lanterns that acted as traffic lights and have long since been removed.

4. Judah Baker Windmill
South Yarmouth

Another historic windmill sits on the grounds of the appropriately named Windmill Park on Bass River. Originally built in 1791 by Judah Baker, it was situated in Dennis until 1866, when it was moved to its current location. It was extensively restored in 1999 and now appears as it did when built more than two hundred years ago. The mill became obsolete with the advent of large commercial mills in the early twentieth century.

Windmill Park, on a small parcel of land alongside Bass River, has a very small swimming area and a great view of boats coming in and out from Nantucket Sound. Nearly the entire length of West Dennis Beach is visible across the river from Windmill Park. The windmill is opened seasonally, and the Yarmouth Historical Commission is happy to provide a schedule for any interested visitors.

Important Info:
• Free parking

JUDAH BAKER WINDMILL

5. Seagull Beach
West Yarmouth

One of two main beaches on the south side of Yarmouth, along with Smuggler's Beach, Seagull Beach is a perfect spot to spend the day. It is bordered on the east by Parkers River and on the west by the private Great Island area. The residents of Great Island are very strict about trespassing, so it is best to pay close attention to the signs designating where the public land ends.

Seagull Beach provides a great view of boats entering and exiting Hyannis Harbor and the aircraft coming in and leaving Barnstable Municipal Airport, as well as Lewis Pond, which lies north of the parking lot.

At the end of the large paved parking lot, there is a short dirt road leading to a small parking lot facing Parkers River, where there is ample room for fishing. Being a very popular beach, the parking areas fill up early during the summer. It is wise to plan accordingly if you want to enjoy this spot.

Important Info:
- Daily parking, $20
- Lifeguards and concessions in season
- No dogs allowed

SEAGULL BEACH IN JULY

GPS: Not provided
Address: Great Island Road, West Yarmouth

6. Point Gammon Lighthouse

Standing stoically silent at the tip of Great Island is this beacon. It helped guide the way for vessels to their destinations from 1816 to 1858, when it was decommissioned in favor of Bishop and Clerks Lighthouse, 3 miles offshore. Today it is the end of the line on the immensely private area known as Great Island. The 25-foot-tall stone lighthouse can be seen from nearby beaches and by boat. However, getting up close and personal is not a suggested option. There are many treacherous boulders around the shore of Great Island, making docking a boat dangerous. Great Island is above all a private community, and it is not recommended to trespass on the property.

POINT
GAMMON
LIGHTHOUSE

7. Baxter Grist Mill
Yarmouth

This piece of history is one of the most viewed spots on the Cape, but probably one of the least noticed. The three-hundred-year-old Baxter Grist Mill sits along a busy section of Rt. 28, close to the Hyannis town line. Thousands of people pass by every day, usually on their way to someplace else. A parking area is just before the actual mill on Mill Pond Road.

Built in 1710 and named for Thomas Baxter, this corn mill is one of several located on Cape Cod. It is still quite easy to imagine the Baxter family grinding corn for several generations before technology made the mill obsolete around 1900, when electricity and commercial flour became more readily available. In the early 1930s, automobile pioneer Henry Ford attempted to purchase the mill but was rejected. He instead had the nearby Farris Windmill purchased and shipped to Michigan.

At one time the mill had a large, wooden waterwheel. It was the first site in Yarmouth named to the National Register of Historic Places. Near the parking area, one of the original turbines used in the mill sits among the pine trees and is the only piece of the mill that can be easily touched. It was completely restored in 2021. There is a chain-link fence surrounding the wooden mill, but it is open seasonally for visitors, and the Yarmouth Historical Commission is glad to give a schedule to anyone interested in it.

Important Info:
• Free parking next to the mill.

BAXTER GRIST MILL

XV

HYANNIS

GPS: (41.6516606592893, -70.28384345212659)
Address: 367 Main Street, Hyannis

1. Hyannis Village Green

In between the bustle of Main Street and South Street is a little slice of green. Currently it is the home of Barnstable Town Hall. In the past it was home to the Hyannis Normal School and later Cape Cod Community College, all in the same brick building. Art festivals, music on the bandstand, and more make up some of what one can experience here. It is also steps from shops and restaurants and can give one a little breather from popular Main Street.

2. Veterans Beach and Kennedy Memorial

Located just past the harbor on Ocean Street, Veterans Beach is a great place to spend the day. The Korean War Memorial and John F. Kennedy Memorial are in Veterans Memorial Park on the beach grounds and provide an extra attraction for visitors. The JFK Memorial consists of a beautiful fountain and a wall with a plaque depicting the late president's profile. The entire area is surrounded by sweet-smelling flowers in the warmer months, including several varieties of roses. The memorial is on a hill where you can see a panoramic view of Lewis Bay and the boats entering and leaving the harbor.

Beside the JFK Memorial is the spectacular Korean War Memorial. The statue of the American soldier stands on a pedestal, looking out over the water. A backdrop of flags includes the American flag flanked by the flags of the United Nations, South Korea, Massachusetts, and POW/MIA. It is a great patriotic attraction that needs to be seen on any trip through Hyannis.

Veterans Beach is next to Hyannis Yacht Club and is sheltered somewhat from the harsh ocean. On the north side of the beach, a river leads to a pond across Ocean Street. This is a great place to see ducks, geese, seagulls, and even crows and hawks congregating. There are swings for the kids and a nice, shady picnic area. Boats, both big and small, pass by frequently, heading into the harbor or out toward Nantucket or the open ocean. Veterans Beach, with some history mixed in, is a wonderful spot for a fun day.

Important Info:
• Daily parking, $25
• Lifeguards and concessions in season
• No dogs allowed

KOREAN WAR MEMORIAL

KENNEDY MEMORIAL

THE RIVER NEXT TO VETERANS BEACH

3. Kalmus Beach

This pristine stretch of beach sits at the entrance to Lewis Bay. It is popular for windsurfing as well as swimming. Due to its proximity to the routes to the islands of Nantucket and Martha's Vineyard, it is possible to see multiple ferries passing by the beach daily. The beach is named after Herbert Kalmus, who played a large part in the development of color motion picture film. Kalmus at one time owned the land upon which the beach stands. This spot is routinely filled with people and cars regardless of the time of year. From swimming in the summer, to picnics in the spring and fall, to winter sunsets, Kalmus is a year-round destination.

Important Info:
• Daily parking: $25

XVI

CENTERVILLE

1. Craigville Beach

One of the most popular beaches on all of Cape Cod, Craigville Beach lies almost in the middle of the southern coast of Cape Cod. The name "Craigville" comes from Dr. J. Austin Craig, who was president of the Christian Biblical Institute until his death in 1881. The beach became popular just after the turn of the twentieth century. It is bordered on the east by the smaller Covell's Beach and on the north by the Centerville River; there are many beautiful private homes along the river. The Kennedy family compound can be seen after a long, eastward walk on the beach. Craigville Beach is

CRAIGVILLE BEACH

a popular starting and finishing point for bike races, road races, and marathons on the Cape and in eastern Massachusetts. It is a warmer-water beach, since it faces Nantucket Sound, and is great for swimming. The long stretch of sand makes it a good area to take a peaceful walk during just about any time of year.

Important Info:
- Daily parking, $25
- Lifeguard and concessions in season
- No dogs allowed

CRAIGVILLE BEACH

2. 1856 Country Store

Built in the 1840s as a storage barn for cranberries, this historic store has been a landmark in Centerville for more than 150 years. To this day the general store sells homemade jams and jellies, soaps, cards, and classic penny candies. It is a trip back into childhood for some older visitors, and perhaps an introduction to something new for younger visitors.

Despite being a part of Cape Cod for so long, the store is keeping up with the times. It is now possible to purchase items on their website (www.1856countrystore.com). The little red store has a homey feel to it and a very friendly, accommodating staff. The separate benches outside

1856 COUNTRY STORE

the front door for "Democrats" and "Republicans" are always good for a chuckle. The 1856 Country Store can be a pit stop during a walk on Centerville's beautiful Main Street or a primary destination. This general store, a Cape Cod institution, is open year-round for all to visit.

Important Info:
• Free parking

1856 COUNTRY STORE

XVIII

COTUIT

GPS: (41.606121, -70.437405)
Address: Oceanview Avenue, Cotuit

1. Loop Beach

With all of the popular and well-known beaches on the south side of Cape Cod, it is easy to miss some incredible spots. Loop Beach, on Ocean View Avenue, is one that could be overlooked. The road is a one-way loop, giving the beach its name. The beach parking area is not very large and sits at the mouth of Cotuit Bay. The beach is nice—about what one would expect on Cape Cod—but the walk up the hill on Ocean View Avenue gives some most-stunning views. The road is dotted with private homes, but several open patches of landscape allow for a view of Cotuit Bay, Oyster Harbors, Nantucket Sound, and Sampson's Island Sanctuary. The elevation of the road gives a perspective on these areas that is tough to match. The climb up the hill is not difficult or very long, and visitors should take a walk during a break from swimming or relaxing at Loop Beach.

Important Info:
- Free parking
- Lifeguard in season
- No concessions
- Dogs allowed Sept. 15 to May 15

Note: It is listed as a "Barnstable Resident's Only" beach, which may restrict it to only year-round residents and those with vacation homes.

THE VIEW FROM OCEAN VIEW
AVENUE NEAR LOOP BEACH

THE VIEW FROM OCEAN VIEW AVENUE NEAR LOOP BEACH

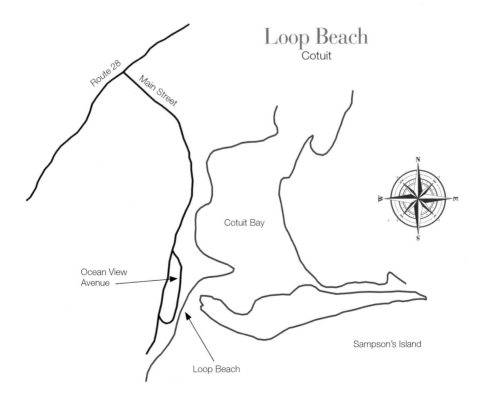

Loop Beach
Cotuit

Route 28

Main Street

Cotuit Bay

Ocean View
Avenue

Loop Beach

Sampson's Island

XVIII

MASHPEE

1. Old Indian Church

The Native American Wampanoag people are synonymous with Cape Cod. They were here before the first Cape settlements and are still a vital part of the Cape today. For a deeper understanding of the Wampanoags, a visit should be paid to the Old Indian Meeting House, also known as the Old Indian Church.

Built around 1684 as a place for the Wampanoags to practice Christianity, the church is the oldest on the Cape. Though the exact date of its construction is debated, it is rightfully considered one of the most historic buildings on the entire Cape. It is generally thought that the Old Indian Church was moved from its original location in 1717 and relocated to its current site, just off Rt. 28 on Meetinghouse Road. A cemetery was built on the grounds in the late eighteenth century, and the building once was used as a school.

The church is still used for services by the Wampanoags. After being closed for six years while it underwent a million-dollar renovation, it was reopened in 2009. This Native American church is one of only a few that remain in Massachusetts. It is also one of only a few historic buildings in Mashpee. This is a must-see place for those with a desire to find out more about the original inhabitants of Cape Cod.

Important Info:
• Free parking

OLD INDIAN CHURCH

2. South Cape Beach State Park

SOUTH CAPE BEACH STATE PARK

This hidden gem of a park is a bit out of the way but is well worth the trip. The park is relatively easy to find from the Mashpee Rotary. From the parking lot there is a view of Martha's Vineyard across Vineyard Sound and the beach, but the beach is only the beginning. There are trails through the wooded areas north of the beach, as well as a trail leading between the beach and Sage Lot Pond. Sage Lot Pond is home to swans and ducks, and the path is an easy walk to the state jetty at the mouth of Waquoit Bay. Boardwalks allow visitors to travel over the dunes without damaging them.

Some believe that Waquoit Bay was the famed Vinland, the first landing place of Viking Leif Ericson a thousand years ago. For nearly a hundred years, many intelligent minds have been trying to prove just that. But whether it is the first landing spot of the Vikings in North America or not, Waquoit Bay is a beautiful, natural place. From the state jetty there is a good look across the mouth of the bay to Washburn Island State Park in East Falmouth.

The park gates are closed from Columbus Day to Patriots Day, but parking can be found at the Mashpee Town Beach at the end of the entrance road.

Important Info:
- Daily admission fee (June 21–September 5) MA resident $15, nonresident $40
- Lifeguards and concessions in season
- Dogs allowed except in swimming areas

SAGE LOT POND

SUNSET AT SOUTH CAPE BEACH STATE PARK

XIX

FALMOUTH & WOODS HOLE

1. Spohr Gardens

Off the beaten path is this 6-acre slice of gardeners' heaven. Known for its thousands of beautiful daffodils and many more species of flowers, it overlooks Oyster Pond. The grounds were developed in the 1950s by Charles and Margaret Spohr. In the spring the Daffodil Days celebration brings out the crowds. It is easy to lose oneself walking the wonderfully manicured paths, standing on the dock, or even gardening. Yes, Spohr Gardens allows volunteers to come and help out with the gardening.

Important Info:
• Free parking; grounds open 8 a.m. to 8 p.m.

2. Nobska Lighthouse
Falmouth

Originally constructed in 1829, the current Nobska Lighthouse was built in 1876 and became a part of the Coast Guard family in 1939. The hill where the lighthouse stands offers a magnificent view of Vineyard Sound, Martha's Vineyard, and the Elizabeth Islands.

From the point on Nobska Road, it is possible to see all the way down into Woods Hole to the west, where ferry boats carry passengers out to Martha's Vineyard quite often throughout the day. Because Nobska Light sits on a hill, photos of this amazing lighthouse can be taken from many angles, each giving a unique viewpoint. There is also a place across the street that gives a wider perspective of the lighthouse, though care must be taken since it sits at the top of a steep dirt hill leading to the rocky shore below. The grounds of the lighthouse are always open to the public, but the lighthouse itself is on Coast Guard grounds. There are free tours of the lighthouse a few times during the summer and again on New Year's Eve, which is a great time to visit, especially if there is snow on the ground.

In 2020 the lighthouse was completely renovated. The keeper's house is in the process of becoming a maritime museum as well.

Important Info:
• Limited free parking in front of lighthouse

NOBSKA LIGHTHOUSE

3. Steamship Authority Ferry to Martha's Vineyard
Woods Hole

From Woods Hole, both Martha's Vineyard and the Elizabeth Islands appear so close that you could reach out and touch them. From the ferry docks, it is barely half a mile across the Sound to the coast of the Elizabeth Islands and a little more than 2 miles to the edge of the Vineyard.

The ships of the Steamship Authority and its predecessors have been sailing the Vineyard Sound waters since 1818. The schedule and rates are reasonable for an island getaway. The typical ferry trip takes roughly forty-five minutes, with at least thirteen voyages beginning from Woods Hole each day, even in the winter.

Another Steamship Authority terminal in Hyannis offers faster access to Nantucket. There are two year-round ports on Martha's Vineyard at Oak Bluffs and Vineyard Haven, and one on Nantucket. In addition there are several seasonal terminals, including ones in New Bedford, Falmouth, and Harwich, to make travel easier.

The Woods Hole terminal was demolished, with a brand-new one finished in mid-2022.

Important Info:
- Daily parking per vehicle (Palmer Avenue lot): April 1 to May 14: $13; May 15 to September 14: $15 (Weekdays) $20 (Weekends); September 15 to October 31: $13; November 1 to March 31: $10

THE OLD STEAMSHIP AUTHORITY TERMINAL BEFORE IT WAS RAZED IN 2018.

ABOARD A FERRY BOUND FOR MARTHA'S VINEYARD.

GPS: (41.525226, -70.672781)
Address: 266 Woods Hole Road, Woods Hole

4. Woods Hole Oceanographic Institute
Woods Hole

Sometimes lost in the majesty of Cape Cod is the fact that it is also home to one of the leading scientific communities on the entire planet. The Woods Hole Oceanographic Institute (WHOI) was established in 1930 and is the largest independent oceanographic institute in the United States.

Many incredible discoveries and historic events have come out of WHOI, including the first manned deep-sea submersible, *Alvin*, which was commissioned in 1964. DSV-*Alvin* is most famous for being the vessel that explored the remains of the *Titanic* in 1986.

WHOI and the Woods Hole community as a whole are open to the public, with many fun and interesting things for visitors to do and see. It is a mix of scientific community, fishing village, and seaside retreat, all of which mesh together seamlessly.

Many small shops and restaurants lining Water Street will keep visitors happy and occupied during their visit—between seal shows at the Woods Hole Aquarium. There is no shortage of entertaining activities in Woods Hole, and, of course, Martha's Vineyard is only a short ferry trip away.

Important Info:

• Limited parking on streets with parking meters. It is possible to park in Falmouth and take the WHOOSH trolley into Woods Hole.

WATER STREET IN WOODS HOLE

WOODS HOLE MARINE BIOLOGICAL LIBRARY

LOOKING ACROSS EEL POND TO WOODS HOLE

GPS: (41.54219742016132, -70.66107706949978)
Address: 71 Quissett Harbor Road, Falmouth

5. The Knob

Located on both Quissett Harbor and Buzzards Bay, this rock formation is all at once hard to find and hard to miss. Popular for picturesque sunset photography and weddings, this natural wonder was gifted to the Salt Pond Areas Bird Sanctuaries by Cornelia Carey upon her death in 1973. The property had been in the Carey family for generations. Before her passing, Cornelia paid to have the Knob armored with rocks to prevent erosion, guaranteeing that future generations would be able to gaze upon its beauty. The half-mile walk out to the Knob is filled with panoramic views and encounters with local wildlife. It is just as satisfying to stand along the shore of Quissett Harbor in the summer and watch the boats coming and going.

THE KNOB IN FALMOUTH

6. Bourne Farm
North Falmouth

Bourne Farm is on the way up Cape Cod's west coast. Established in 1775, it has a spectacular view of the sloping green hill leading down to Crocker Pond, in addition to the historic buildings on the property. The 49-acre farm is perfect for hiking or walking dogs and is available for weddings and other events. The farmhouse itself, known as the Crowell-Bourne Farmhouse, was erected by Joseph Crowell with his father. The Salt Pond Areas Bird Sanctuaries oversees Bourne Farm and handles rentals of the grounds and barn for special occasions. This is a good

BOURNE FARM

place to escape for a few hours and is well worth seeking out on your travels. There is even an old cattle tunnel that takes you underneath the Shining Sea Bikeway.

Important Info:
• Free parking on-site

CROCKER POND
AT BOURNE FARM

GPS: (41.623286, -70.639163)
Address: 350 Quaker Road, North Fallmouth

7. Old Silver Beach
North Falmouth

Old Silver Beach is one of the best-known places on the west coast of Cape Cod. On Quaker Road in North Falmouth, it is popular with locals, who fill the parking lot daily during the summer. Two parking areas are on either side of a salt marsh that empties into the bay, and a pair of jetties divide the beach in half. The beach is so busy that there is a special lane on the Quaker Road approach that is specifically for the backup of cars waiting to pay to get in during the summer.

The views of the marsh on the east, Buzzards Bay on the west, and the Cleveland Ledge Light in the distance are simply amazing. The lighthouse sits far out in the water yet peeks over the horizon due to its immense size. The bayside waters are warmer, with stronger currents.

During the 1920s the University Players—including Margaret Sullavan, James Stewart, and Henry Fonda—performed here for several years. The theater where they performed burned down in the 1930s.

It is easy to see why so many people plan to visit Old Silver Beach when coming to Cape Cod.

Important Info:
- Daily parking, $30
- Lifeguards and concessions in season
- Dogs allowed October 1 to April 30

CLEVELAND LEDGE LIGHTHOUSE FROM OLD SILVER BEACH

OLD SILVER BEACH

8. Cleveland Ledge Lighthouse
Falmouth

The last lighthouse built in New England, Cleveland Ledge Light was named for former president Grover Cleveland, who fished the waters of Buzzards Bay. Completed in 1943, the lighthouse sits 2 miles off shore on a 52-foot-tall concrete pillar. It was maintained by the Coast Guard but in 2010 was purchased by Sandy Boyd of California, who is planning to restore it to its original condition.

It is best viewed from shore and cannot be climbed. There are several places to see this enormous light station along the Falmouth coast, with the best public views probably from Old Silver Beach.

Important Info:
• Best viewed from Old Silver Beach

CLEVELAND LEDGE LIGHTHOUSE FROM OLD SILVER BEACH

GPS: North End (41.647972, -70.613804)
South End (41.522993, -70.669063)
Address: Begins on County Road

9. Shining Sea Bikeway
Falmouth

A separate but equally scenic and beautiful part of Cape Cod's bike trails, the Shining Sea Bikeway takes its name from a line in the iconic "America the Beautiful," written by Katharine Lee Bates, a Falmouth resident. The nearly 11-mile-long trail was opened in 1975 and is an easy ride. It goes along the shore of Woods Hole into Falmouth, affording riders, runners, and walkers some incredible views of Martha's Vineyard and Vineyard Sound. Once through Woods Hole and Falmouth, the bike trail goes past West Falmouth Harbor and Bourne Farm and runs close to Old Silver Beach. It ends in North Falmouth, where the main parking area is on County Road, just after Rt. 151.

There are small parking areas along the trail for those who wish to start where they please. Shining Sea Bikeway may not be as long as the other bike trails on Cape Cod, but the views it offers more than make up for its diminutive length. There is a sense of accomplishment when a rider covers its entire length, which is much easier to complete than the Cape Cod Rail Trail.

Important Info:
- Free parking all along the bike path
- Concessions in season at north and south ends

THE SEMISECRET BEGINNING OF THE SHINING SEA BIKEWAY ON COUNTY ROAD

XX

POCASSET

1. Wings Neck Lighthouse

Positioned inches from the water on Wings Neck Island in Pocasset is Wings Neck Lighthouse, now part of a private home available for vacation rentals. The original lighthouse was built in 1849, but damage from a fire caused a new lighthouse to be built in 1889. The view of the Atlantic Ocean and Buzzards Bay from Wings Neck is incredible. Once the Cape Cod Canal was constructed, water traffic around the Wings Neck Light area increased, and it became very important to the safety of traveling vessels near the tip of Wings Neck, which sticks a mile and a half out into Buzzards Bay.

The lighthouse was deactivated in 1945 after the construction of nearby Cleveland Ledge Lighthouse. It was put up for sale in 1947 and bought by the Flanagan family of Boston. It is now a three-bedroom, 1.5-bath Airbnb vacation rental. If not renting it, one can see it quite well from the gated opening on the edge of the property, and it is well worth the drive out.

In another interesting twist, the assistant lighthouse keeper's residence, now a private home, was originally a part of Ned's Point Lighthouse in Mattapoisett. In 1923 the house was picked up and floated across Buzzards Bay to Wings Neck.

Important Info:
- Free parking outside the private property

WINGS NECK LIGHTHOUSE

WINGS NECK LIGHTHOUSE

THE ASSISTANT KEEPER'S HOUSE ON THE LEFT, FORMERLY AT NED'S POINT LIGHTHOUSE

XXI

MONUMENT BEACH

1. Monks Park

Located in the small village of Monument Beach, Little Bay Conservation Area is also known as Monks Park. The parking area is bisected by railroad tracks that pass over the dirt road. From these tracks one gets a panoramic view of tree-covered peninsulas to the left and right. It is also an amazing place to watch the sun set as it drops perfectly between the peninsulas.

The peninsula to the left is larger and has a bench and picnic table, enabling you to enjoy views of Buzzards Bay and a few small islands that make up some of Monument Beach. From the tip of this peninsula, the railroad bridge is clearly visible to the northeast and the photo opportunities are endless.

The village of Monument Beach got its name from the Algonquin word "manomet." It became a popular summer resort in 1881, after a railroad line opened nearby that linked this area to New York, New Haven, and Hartford.

Important Info:
• Free parking
• No lifeguard
• No concessions

LITTLE BAY
CONSERVATION
AREA

THE RAILROAD BRIDGE
SEEN FROM THE LITTLE BAY
CONSERVATION AREA

SUNSET AT THE LITTLE
BAY CONSERVATION
AREA

Little Bay Conservation Area
Monument Beach

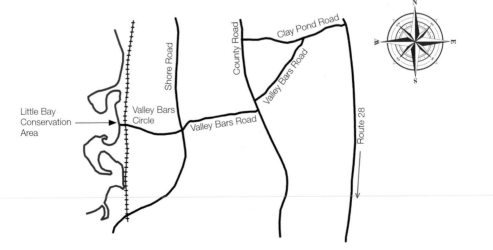

Little Bay
Conservation
Area

Shore Road

County Road

Clay Pond Road

Valley Bars
Circle

Valley Bars Road

Valley Bars Road

Route 28

XXII

BOURNE

1. Mashnee Island

Possibly the least known island on Cape Cod, Mashnee Island is not really an island at all, since it is connected by an access road. There are signs for the "island" at the Bourne Rotary, near the bridge, but many people miss them as they head on and off the Cape on the highway. If you follow the signs, you will be led down Mashnee Road, which leads over a sandy spit out to the island itself. There are no places to park on the access road, so one must drive all the way out before seeing the unique community.

Unfortunately, it is basically a residential community with nowhere to park. Visitors to the beaches are generally dropped off, then picked up later. There are a few rentals available on Airbnb.

From the beaches one can see the smoky-gray railroad bridge standing tall behind the treeline, only a little over a mile away. There is also a clear view of the wind turbine at the Massachusetts Maritime Academy, across the Cape Cod Canal. A walk on the beach at Mashnee Island is a beautiful and unexpected experience. Many visitors do not even know this little finger of land stretching out into Buzzards Bay exists, and it is not an easy place to visit because of the lack of parking or conveniences. The view, however, is worth the effort.

THE VIEW FROM MASHNEE ISLAND

Mashnee Island
Buzzards Bay

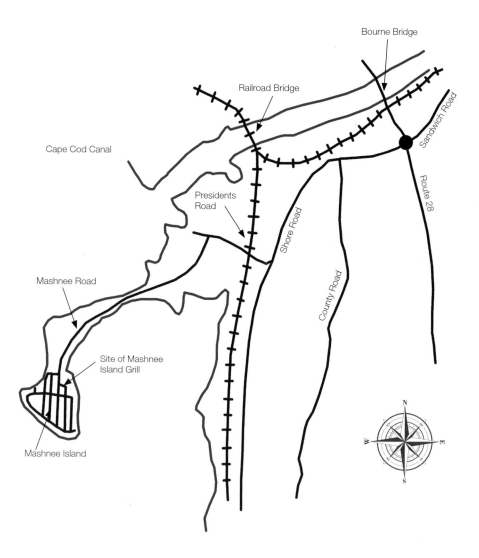

Bourne Bridge

Railroad Bridge

Cape Cod Canal

Sandwich Road

Route 28

Presidents Road

Shore Road

Mashnee Road

County Road

Site of Mashnee Island Grill

Mashnee Island

N
W   E
S

2. Cape Cod Canal Railroad Bridge

The third bridge along the Cape Cod Canal, the Railroad Bridge is a sight to behold. Easy to find by following Shore Road to Bell Road, this bridge is at the end of the paved canal biking and walking path. There are two parking lots near the bridge: a small one almost directly under it and a larger one across the water from the Massachusetts Maritime Academy. This parking lot is at the mouth of the canal, and there are always flocks of birds trying to feed on fish caught in the rapidly moving tides.

The Railroad Bridge, crossing the Canal near Buzzards Bay, was the largest vertical lift bridge in history when it was built in 1935. When raised it has a clearance of 135 feet. Seeing it in action is not easy, since train traffic is not as frequent as it used to be. The main stretch of the bridge sits high above the water unless a train is approaching. However, there is always a chance of seeing a boat or several boats passing by. Whether tiny sailboats or gigantic barges, there is always traffic on the canal.

Important Info:
• Free parking

THE RAILROAD BRIDGE ACROSS THE CAPE COD CANAL

THE RAILROAD BRIDGE ACROSS THE CAPE COD CANAL

A SHIP PASSING BY THE RAILROAD BRIDGE

3. Aptucxet Trading Post & Gray Gables Railroad Station

The Windmill Gift Shop ushers you on a trip back nearly four hundred years. Built in 1627, this was the first trading post used by the fledgling Plymouth Colony. The building that stands is a replica of the original, but the museum houses excavated pieces of the original building. A replica saltworks is located on the grounds as well, consisting of two wooden buildings used to evaporate water from the salt, using the sun.

The windmill at the entrance to the trading post was formerly on the grounds of nineteenth-century actor Joseph Jefferson, friend and fishing companion of President Grover Cleveland. The Gray Gables railroad station sits across from the windmill. It was created for President

Cleveland, whose summer home in Bourne was named Gray Gables. Beginning in 1892, it was the first Cape Cod summer White House.

The station is the original, not a replica, and has a regal flair to it, with its golden color fit for a president. The building was moved to the Aptucxet grounds in 1976. With the canal in sight, this is a nice, shady spot to enjoy.

Important Info:
- Free parking
- Museum entrance fees: adults, $6; children (6–18) $24; Seniors/Military $5
- Open Memorial Day– Columbus Day

THE WINDMILL AT THE ENTRANCE TO THE APTUCXET TRADING POST

APTUCXET TRADING POST

THE SALTWORKS AT THE APTUCXET TRADING POST

THE APTUCXET TRADING POST WITH GRAY GABLES IN THE BACKGROUND

GRAY GABLES STATION

4. Bourne Recreation Area

The Bourne Recreation Area can be hard to find despite the thousands of people who pass directly over it every day. The connector road that runs between the Bourne and Sagamore Bridges is the key. As you approach the Bourne Bridge, stay on Sandwich Road and go under the bridge. Just on the other side a road goes to the left, toward the canal. There is parking on the right.

Picnic tables, where people can eat or just relax, are in the shadow of the massive steel bridge. You can walk along the canal while listening to the rush of highway traffic passing overhead. It is a soothing sort of hum mixed with the gentle lapping of waves on the rocks.

Active railroad tracks pass along the canal and should be carefully watched in case trains come along. The bike path can be used for walking, and on warmer days it is a busy place, with high numbers of bicyclists, runners, and skaters. The bike path is also an access road for government vehicles, but no other motorized traffic. It runs the entire 7-to-8-mile length of the canal. This lesser-known area has a perfect mix of highway bustle and quiet solitude that should be experienced by any visitor to Cape Cod.

Important Info:
• Free parking

BOURNE BRIDGE AT THE BOURNE RECREATION AREA

BOURNE RECREATION AREA

Address: Head back out to Sandwich Road, follow it 0.2 miles. Take a sharp right onto Rt. 6A. Follow it 0.2 miles; take the first exit at the rotary for the Bourne Bridge. I hope you enjoyed your trip around Cape Cod. Please, come back anytime!

LEAVING THE CAPE

BOURNE BRIDGE AT THE BOURNE RECREATION AREA

THE BOURNE BRIDGE FROM BEHIND THE APTUCXET TRADING POST

BIBLIOGRAPHY

Albright, E.J. "Tony Costa." Criminal Minds Wiki. Accessed January 16, 2023. https://criminalminds.fandom.com/wiki/Tony_Costa.

Barnstable Historical Society. "The Old Jail – Barnstable Historical Society." Barnstable Historical Society, barnstablehistoricalsociety.org/the-old-jail/. Accessed 17 Jan. 2023.

Daniels, Clarence B. "That Was the Island That Was" *Cape Cod Compass*, 1964.

1856 Country Store. http://www.1856countrystore.com/.

Falmouth Historical Society—Falmouth Museums on the Green. 2009. https://museumsonthegreen.org/.

Green, Eugene. *Names of the Land.* Chester, CT: Globe Pequot, 1982.

Heritage Museums and Gardens Celebrating the American Spirit. http://www.heritagemuseumsandgardens.org/.

The Historical Society of Old Yarmouth. http://www.hsoy.org.

"HOME." Highlandlighthouse, www.highlandlighthouse.org/. Accessed 17 Jan. 2023.

"Marconi's Wellfleet (Cape Cod) Wireless—Stormfax®." Marconi's Wellfleet Wireless—Stormfax. 2003. http://www.stormfax.com/wireless.htm.

New England Lighthouses: A Virtual Guide—Photos, History, Tours, Cruises, Coastal Accommodations and More. http://www.newenglandlighthouses.net/.

"Old Bourne Village, Bourne Historical Society, Bourne, Cape Cod, MA." Bourne Historical Society, Bourne, Cape Cod, MA. 2008. https://bournehistoricalsociety.org/.

Pilgrim Monument and Museum—Home. 2009. http://pilgrim-monument.org/.

INDEX

ACKNOWLEDGMENTS

I could not have completed this book without the love and support of so many people. Thanks to my family: Mom, Dad, Serpa, Kate, Matt, Lindsay, and Ashley; my Aunts Susie, Kelly, Amy, and Emma; my Uncles Eric, Bob, Steve, and John; my cousins, nieces, and nephews (Kaleigh, Emma, Liam, Landon, Lucas, and Sylvie); and Nina and Grampa, and my Nana, all looking down from heaven. Thanks also to my friends Meg, Barry, John, Deanna, Mike, Steve, Crystal, Adam, Shayna, Dawn, Monique, and KO. A part of each of you is in this book! I have been truly blessed.

SUNSET AT BOUND BROOK ISLAND, WELLFLEET